Praise for *Heavy*

"Oh my god. *Heavy* is astonishing. Difficult. Intense. Layered. Wow. Just wow."

—Roxane Gay, author of *Hunger*

"What I have always loved about Kiese Laymon is that he is as beautiful a person as he is a writer. What he manages to do in the space of a sentence is unparalleled, and that's because no one else practices the art of revision as an act of love quite like Kiese. He loves his mother, his grandmama, Mississippi, black folks, his students, his peers, and anyone else willing to embrace his love enough to give us this gorgeous memoir, *Heavy*. This reckoning with trauma, terror, fear, sexual violence, abuse, addiction, family, secrets, lies, truth, and the weight of the nation and his body would be affecting in less capable hands, but with Kiese at the helm it is nothing short of a modern classic. These sentences that he so painstakingly crafted are some the most arresting ever printed in the English language. Kiese's heart and humor shine through, and we are blessed to have such raw humanity rendered in prose that begs for repeat readings. We do not deserve *Heavy*. We do not deserve Kiese. That he is generous enough to share is testament to his commitment to helping us all heal."

—Mychal Denzel Smith, author of
Invisible Man, Got the Whole World Watching

"There are those rare writers in the world whose work unearths the stories that have been buried in and around us for so long. They force us to confront all that we would rather not see, and ask us to reckon with why we have failed to see it for so long. Kiese Laymon is one such rare writer. *Heavy* is a memoir, yes, but it is also a testament to a sort of truth and self-reflection that is increasingly rare in our world today. If for some reason you were not already convinced, there should no longer be any doubt that Kiese Laymon is one of the important writers of our time."

—Clint Smith, author of *Counting Descent*

"At once tender and explosive, Kiese Laymon's *Heavy* is a growing-up story laden with an unusual candor. The book is stark, beautiful, challenging, and refreshing. Laymon explores abuse, love, violence, addiction, gender, and race without ever veering into the realm of the titillating or dehumanizing. He carries his people with a sweetness and fullness of heart that allows them to shine in three dimensions, allowed to be ugly and complicated and beloved and human. The abundance of *Heavy* is going to be a gift for many hurting hearts, in our time and beyond."

—Eve Ewing, author of *Electric Arches*

"With *Heavy*, Laymon has outlined the wretched shape of our relentless national lie with duty and precision, breathing and pouring into it to shine the light ever brighter on its contours and limits. *Heavy* is an intimate excavation, a diagnosis, and a prescription for a cure for the terrifying dishonesty of the American body politic. I did not want to remember what I have found necessary to forget. Ready or not, *Heavy* remembers for me, and for us all, with the exquisite black southern precision of a post-soul blues. Its brilliance is in its intimate and firm reminder that we are more than what has been done to us by others and by this nation, and that we can and must unburden ourselves as we move toward freedom. With *Heavy*, Laymon, the chief blues scribe of our time, writes and plays us a path through the weight of things."

—Zandria F. Robinson,
author of *This Ain't Chicago*

"Kiese Laymon's new book is an emotional powerhouse. He fearlessly takes the reader into the dark corners of his interior life. Wound, grief, and enduring pain reside there. But this

book is a love letter. And, as we all know, love is a beautiful *and* funky experience. Thank you, Kiese, for this gift."
—Eddie Glaude, author of *Democracy in Black*

"Kiese Laymon has done nothing less than write the autobiography of the first generation of African Americans born after the civil rights movement of the 1960s and the black power ethos of the 1970s. His story of grappling with love and violence and language and our bodies is this generation's story, and it is as moving and heartbreaking and heartwarming as you would expect. And then some."
—Courtney Baker, author of *Humane Insight*

"*Heavy* is an act of truth telling unlike any other I can think of in American literature, partly due to Laymon's uniquely gifted mind—his ability to pursue the ways we lie to each other while also loving each other, or not, and the humility he brings to bear while doing so, this consistently brings us back to life, to what matters in this world. *Heavy* is a gift to us, if we can pick it up—a moral exercise and an intimate history that is at the same time a story about America."
—Alexander Chee, author of
How to Write an Autobiographical Novel

"On the low, many in these United States of America imagine that to be black means that whiteness, whether in its feigned supremacy or brutal imaginings, should be the center of every black story. But nah, that's meager. In *Heavy*, Kiese Laymon remembers how people who loved each other or might have loved each other nearly shattered everything around them with hurt and then struggled to piece it all back together. Kiese crafts the most honest and intimate account of growing up black and southern since Richard Wright's *Black Boy*. Circumventing the myths about blackness, he writes something as complex and fragile as who we is. An insider's look into the making of a writer, *Heavy* is part memoir and part look into the books that turned a kid into a storyteller. *Heavy* invites us into a black South that remembers that we loved each other through it all. In 'Nikki-Rosa,' Nikki Giovanni wrote that 'black love is black wealth.' This book is the weight of black love, and might we all be wealthy by daring to open up to it."

—Reginald Dwayne Betts,
author of *A Question of Freedom*

"*Heavy* heaves, sings, hums, and runs all night to make it clear that there's an alternative, that black history's first premise is mutuality. That mutuality isn't perfect, ain't safe, it's danger-ous, in fact, and *Heavy* moves in a terrible and beautiful and so gentle proximity to that—at crucial times our primary—danger, the ones we love and who love us the most. I was with Kiese the whole damn heavy-floating way, word for word in laughter and tears, in recognition, refraction, and revelation. But, way more than any of those, sentence by sentence, I was with Kiese in thanks."

—Ed Pavlić, author of *Another Kind of Madness*

"In *Heavy*, Kiese Laymon asks how to survive in a body despite the many violences that are inflicted upon it: the vio-lence of racism, of misogyny, of history—the violence of a culture that treats the bodies of black men with fear and sus-picion more often than with tenderness and attentive care. In prose that sears at the same time as it soars, Kiese Laymon breaks the unbearable silence each of these violences, in their peculiar cruelty, has imposed. Permeated with humility, brav-ery, and a bold intersectional feminism, *Heavy* is a triumph. I stand in solidarity with this book, and with its writer."

—Lacy M. Johnson, author of
The Other Side and *The Reckonings*

"How appropriate Kiese Laymon's stunning memoir is titled *Heavy*. Not only are the stains and hurt highlighted here, heavy, but also the writer's capacity to revive graveyards of ghosts who haunt and seemingly will continue to haunt the protagonist. Laymon is a fearless writer, our writer, who's willing to expose and explore his most vulnerable interiors so that we might get closer to our truths. This is a southern book for backroads and cornbread, for Cadillacs and collard greens, for big mamas and moonshine. *Heavy* is full of our beautiful and ugly histories, and a declaration of how we might seek redemption. The colorful and complicated characters here speak a blues and poetry that is both nostalgic and familiar. This is the book we need right now. We should all be thankful for this ultramodern weighty testament of heartache, catharsis, and utter brilliance."

—Derrick Harriell, author of
Stripper in Wonderland and *Ropes*

"You do not just read Kiese Laymon's work. It does a reading of you, too—one that unburies the stories you thought you would never be able to tell truthfully, and reminds you of your voice to tell them. *Heavy* marks this quality in its highest definition yet. Written with as much devastating poignance as a humor only the black South could inspire, *Heavy* asks readers not just to observe Laymon's courageous journey to understand even the most frightening complexities of life in an antiblack, sexist, fatphobic society, but to embark on it with him. In doing so, Laymon's gorgeous wordsmithing moves us beyond simple binaries of pleasure and pain, joy and trauma, toward a deeper love for communities too often flattened into one dimension. *Heavy* is a book for the ages."

—Hari Ziyad, author of *Black Boy Out of Time*

"*Heavy* is beautiful, lyrical, painful, and really brave. It is both exigent and timeless. Laymon's use of juxtaposition—of the political and personal, the many stories of dishonesty and history, violence, everything—is all-world."

—Nafissa Thompson-Spires, author of
Heads of the Colored People

ALSO BY KIESE LAYMON

Long Division: A Novel

*How to Slowly Kill Yourself
and Others in America: Essays*

HEAVY

AN AMERICAN MEMOIR

KIESE LAYMON

SCRIBNER

New York   London   Toronto   Sydney   New Delhi

Scribner
An Imprint of Simon & Schuster, Inc.
1230 Avenue of the Americas
New York, NY 10020

First Scribner hardcover edition October 2018

SCRIBNER and design are registered trademarks of The Gale Group, Inc., used under license by Simon & Schuster, Inc., the publisher of this work.

For information about special discounts for bulk purchases, please contact Simon & Schuster Special Sales at 1-866-506-1949 or business@simonandschuster.com.

The Simon & Schuster Speakers Bureau can bring authors to your live event. For more information or to book an event contact the Simon & Schuster Speakers Bureau at 1-866-248-3049 or visit our website at www.simonspeakers.com.

Manufactured in the United States of America

3   5   7   9   10   8   6   4

Library of Congress Control Number: 2018002915

ISBN 978-1-5011-2565-2
ISBN 978-1-5011-2569-0 (ebook)

For the porch that Grandmama built

. . . cause wholeness is no trifling matter. A lot of weight when you're well.

—Toni Cade Bambara, *The Salt Eaters*

CONTENTS

CONTENTS

BEEN

I did not want to write to you. I wanted to write a lie. I did not want to write honestly about black lies, black thighs, black loves, black laughs, black foods, black addictions, black stretch marks, black dollars, black words, black abuses, black blues, black belly buttons, black wins, black beens, black bends, black consent, black parents, or black children. I did not want to write about us. I wanted to write an American memoir.

I wanted to write a lie.

I wanted to do that old black work of pandering and lying to folk who pay us to pander and lie to them every day. I wanted to write about our families' relationships to simple carbohydrates, deep-fried meats, and high-fructose corn syrup. I wanted the book to begin with my weighing 319 pounds and end with my weighing 165 pounds. I wanted to pepper the book with acerbic warnings to us fat black folk in the Deep South and saccharine sentimental exhortations from Grandmama. I did not want you to laugh.

I wanted to write a lie.

I wanted to write about how fundamental present black fathers, responsible black mothers, magical black grandmothers, and perfectly disciplined black children are to our liberation. I wanted to center a something, a someone who wants us dead and dishonest. I wanted white Americans, who have proven themselves even more unwilling to confront their lies, to reconsider how their lies limit our access to good love, healthy choices, and second chances. I wanted the book to begin and end with the assumption that if white Americans reckoned with their insatiable appetites for black American suffering, and we reckoned with our insatiable appetites for unhealthy food, we could all be ushered into a reformed era of American prosperity. I wanted to create a fantastic literary spectacle. I wanted that literary spectacle to ask nothing of you, Grandmama, or me other than our adherence to a low-carb diet, limited sugar, weight lifting, twelve thousand steps a day, gallons of water, and no eating after midnight. I wanted you to promise. I did not want you to remember.

I wanted to write a lie.

I wanted that lie to be titillating.

I wrote that lie.

It was titillating.

You would have loved it.

I discovered nothing.

You would have loved it.

I started over and wrote what we hoped I'd forget.

I was eleven years old, five-nine, 208 pounds when you told me to stand still and act like your husband. You'd just given me your daddy's musty brown brim, five dollars, and the directive to play the slot machine next to yours. We were under the stars on the Vegas Strip celebrating the only Christmas we'd ever spent away from Grandmama's shotgun house in Forest, Mississippi. Instead of sliding my five dollars in the machine, I put the money in the pocket of my Raiders Starter jacket. After four pulls, I remember 260 quarters splashing the tin catcher in front of you. We looked over our right shoulders. We looked over our left shoulders. We got on our knees. We raked more quarters than I'd ever seen into that warped white cup.

"Rake, Kie," you said. "Rake."

I loved how you used "rake" to describe what we were doing. When you wrapped my hand in yours and told me to hold the cup steady, I was convinced that we were the luckiest black couple in Las Vegas. Even though you were winning, even though we'd just won, you did not look at me. You kept pulling that handle and looking behind you. "Just one more minute," you said. "I think I can hit again. I promise. Just one more minute."

Every time you promised, I believed you.

I told Grandmama about all the quarters we raked when we got back to Aunt Linda's apartment that night. Grandmama didn't say a word. She looked her twitching eyes past me, found your eyes, and said, "Is that right? You know didn't nan one of them casinos build themselves. They all built off of some fool's money."

You slept on a slender pallet that night in Vegas. I was supposed to be sleeping next to you but I couldn't because I was so happy. Your snores reminded me that you were alive. If you were alive and next to me, I had everything in the world I could ever want.

When we got back from Vegas, you used some of those quarters in the warped white cup to buy an extra tennis racket. The first time we played at Callaway High School, we were volleying when the sound of an M-80 distracted us. We looked toward the school and saw a black woman in a faded jean jacket on one knee. She was wiping the blood from her nose in front of a slender black man in a short blue Members Only jacket.

"Put them hands down," we heard the man say. The woman in the faded jean jacket slowly dropped her hands and the man hit her in the face with what sounded like a loose soggy fist. The woman in the faded jean jacket fell to the ground, murmured something to the man, and covered her face.

Without saying a word, we cocked our rackets and sprinted toward the couple. "Motherfucker," you screamed as the man pulled the woman up. "You better not hit her again, mother-fucker." When the man saw us coming after him, he dragged the woman off through the dirt path.

"Motherfucker," I yelled, and looked for confirmation that cussing in front of you was okay. On the other side of the building, the man, and the woman in the faded jean jacket whose face he'd exploded, got in a raggedy black Mazda. She put on her seat belt and they sped off. We didn't call the police. We didn't run back to our Nova.

We caught our breath.

We held hands.

We got on our knees.

I'd never prayed in the middle of that kind of anger, or fear. I knew we were praying for the safety of the woman in the jean jacket. I assumed we were also praying for ourselves. If we could have touched the man, he would have suffered.

We would have killed him.

I realized that day we didn't simply love each other. We were of two vastly different generations of blackness, but I was your child. We had the same husky thighs, short arms, full cheeks, mushy insides, and minced imagination. We were excellent at working until our bodies gave out, excellent at laughing and laughing and laughing until we didn't. We were excellent at hiding and misdirecting, swearing up and down we were naked when we were fully clothed. Our heart meat was so thick. Once punctured, though, we waltzed those hearts into war without a plan of escape. No matter how terrified or hurt we were, we didn't dare ask anybody for help. We stewed. We remembered. We heaved like two hulks. We resented everyone who watched us suffer. We strapped ourselves in for the next disaster, knowing—though we had no proof—we would always recover.

As a child, on nights when you and I didn't sleep together, I remember trembling, imagining a life where I wasn't yours. I remember you chiding me not to use contractions when talking to white people and police. I remember believing all your lies were mistakes, and forgetting those mistakes when we woke up tucked into each other. Every time you said my particular kind of hardheadedness and white Mississippians' brutal desire for black suffering were recipes for an early death, institutionalization, or incarceration, I knew you were right.

I just didn't care.

I cared about the way you'd grit your teeth when you beat me for not being perfect. I cared about girls at school seeing my welts. I cared about you. Days, and often hours, before you beat me, you touched me so gently. You told me you loved me. You called me your best friend. You forgave me for losing the key to the house. You coated the ashy cracks in my face with Vaseline-slick palms. You used your nubby thumbs, wet with saliva, to clean the sleep out of my eyes. You made me feel like the most beautiful black boy in the history of Mississippi until you didn't.

"I didn't try to hurt you," you told me the last time we

spoke. "I don't remember hurting you as much as you remember being hurt, Kie. I'm not saying it didn't happen. I'm just saying I don't remember everything the way you do."

I still believe you.

This summer, it took one final conversation with Grandmama for me to understand that no one in our family—and very few folk in this nation—has any desire to reckon with the weight of where we've been, which means no one in our family—and very few folk in this nation—wants to be free. I asked Grandmama why she stayed in Mississippi instead of running to the Midwest with the rest of her family if white folk made her so sick, and why she told so many of her stories in present tense.

"The land, Kie," she said. "We work too hard on this land to run. Some of us, we believe the land will one day be free. I been eating off this land my whole life. Greens. Tomatoes. Cucumbers. Collards. You hear me? That's all I can tell you. As far as these stories, I just try to gather up all the gumption I can before I take it to the Lord. And when I tell it to my children, sometimes I just be trying to put y'all where I been."

I wondered, for a second, about why "be trying" and "where I been" felt far heavier than "I try" and "what I have experienced." I asked if I could ask one more difficult question. Grandmama looked at me, for the first time in our lives, like she was afraid. She grabbed her keys and made me wheel her around to the side of the house under the thick scent of her pecan tree. Once we got there, I knelt and asked whether she minded if we talked about words, memory, emergencies, weight, and sexual violence in our family.

Grandmama rubbed the graying hair sliding out from under her wig and put both palms across her frown lines. I asked her why she covered her face when she got nervous or when she laughed. I asked why she wore that fake-looking wig all the time.

"Choices," she murmured. "I already told you. I can't let no man, not even my grandbaby, choose my choice for me." Grandmama looked past what was left of our woods. "Kie, I think we remembered enough for today. I know you been trying to talk about that thing going on thirty years. I need to talk about something else first."

Right there, in the same spot where I remember Grandmama teaching me how to hang up clothes on the clothesline, she told me about not being able to vote, not pissing where she needed to piss, not eating what she needed to eat, not walking how she needed to walk, not driving when she needed to drive because she was born a poor black girl in Scott County, Mississippi. She talked about the shame of white-folk wants always trumping black-folk needs. She talked about how much she loved eating vegetables off her land, and the fear of running north with the rest of her family during the Great Migration. Grandmama told me survival stories placed in offices, washrooms, Sunday school classrooms, parking lots, kitchens, fields, and bedrooms. She told me stories featuring her body and the white foremen at the chicken plant. She told me about Mr. Mumford, about the deacons at our church, about the men who worked the line with her. She told me stories about her father, her uncles, her cousins, and her husband. "I think the men folk forgot," she said near the end, "that I was somebody's child."

Grandmama's body just started laughing. And my body laughed, too. "I'm black and I'm a woman," she finally said. "I love me some Jesus. That's who I always been. And I ain't afraid to shoot somebody trying to harm me and mines. You hear me? I am okay because I pray every day. Some days, the tears just be pouring out my eyes, Kie. But Grandmama is too heavy to blow away or drown in tears made because somebody didn't see me as a somebody worth respecting. You hear me? Ain't nothing in the world worse than looking at your children drowning, knowing ain't nothing you can do because you scared that if you get to trying to save them, they might see that you can't swim either. But I am okay. You hear me?"

I heard Grandmama. But I saw and smelled what diabetes left of her right foot. Grandmama hadn't felt her foot, controlled her bowels, or really tasted her food in over a decade. This Sunday, like every Sunday before it, Grandmama wanted me to know it could all be so much worse. Like you, Grandmama beat the worst of white folk and the mean machinations of men every day she was alive, but y'all taught me indirectly that unacknowledged scars accumulated in battles won often hurt more than battles lost.

"I believe you," I told her. "I will always believe you even when I know you lying." I asked Grandmama if she'd been saying B-E-N-D or B-E-E-N all day.

"Been," she said. "B-E-E-N. Like where you been. And after all the places you and your mama been, y'all way more than mother and son and y'all done way more drowning than an' one of y'all want to admit."

Grandmama was right and Grandmama was wrong.

You and I have never been a family of cabinets filled with Band-Aids, alcohol, and peroxide. We have never been a family of tuck-ins and bedtime stories any more than we've been a family of consistent bill money, pantries, full refrigerators, washers and dryers. We have always been a bent black southern family of laughter, outrageous lies, and books. The presence of all those books, all that laughter, all our lies, and your insistence I read, reread, write, and revise in those books, made it so I would never be intimidated or easily impressed by words, punctuation, sentences, paragraphs, chapters, and white space. You gave me a black southern laboratory to work with words. In that space, I learned how to assemble memory and imagination when I most wanted to die.

Your gifts of reading, rereading, writing, and revision are why I started this book thirty years ago on Grandmama's porch. In spite of those gifts, or maybe because of those gifts, it's important for me to accept, that like all American children, I've been brutally dishonest with you. And like all American parents, you've been brutally dishonest with me.

A few months ago, I was standing behind you with ten dollars I stole from a scared black woman who would never steal ten dollars from me. You were sitting in front of a slot machine, looking nervously over both shoulders, as you spent your last bill money. We were sixteen hundred miles from home. You did not know I was there. If you turned around, I knew you'd talk about how much weight I'd gained, not where our bodies had been since we'd last seen each other.

I wanted to tap you on your shoulder and ask if you were ready to go home. On the way home, I wanted to ask you if we were deserving of different kinds of liberation, different modes of memory, different policy, different practices, and different relationships to honesty. I wanted to ask you if we were also deserving of different books. I am writing a different book to you because books, for better and worse, are how we got here, and I am afraid of speaking any of this to your face.

9

I would try to kill anyone who harmed or spoke ill of you. You would try to kill anyone who harmed or spoke ill of me. But neither of us would ever, under any circumstance, be honest about yesterday. This is how we are taught to love in America. Our dishonesty, cowardice, and misplaced self-righteousness, far more than how much, or how little we weigh is part of why we are suffering. In this way, and far too many others, we are studious children of this nation. We do not have to be this way.

I wanted to write a lie.

You wanted to read that lie.

I wrote this to you instead.

I.

BOY MAN.

TRAIN

You stood in a West Jackson classroom teaching black children how correct usage of the word "be" could save them from white folk while I knelt in North Jackson, preparing to steal the ID card of a fifteen-year-old black girl named Layla Weathersby. I was twelve years old, three years younger than Layla, who had the shiniest elbows, wettest eyes, and whitest Filas of any of us at Beulah Beauford's house. Just like the big boys, Dougie and me, all Layla ever wanted to do was float in the deep end.

Beulah Beauford's house, which sat deep in a North Jackson neighborhood next to ours, was only the second house I'd been in with new encyclopedias, two pantries filled with name-brand strawberry Pop-Tarts, and an in-ground pool. Unlike us in our rented house, which we shared with thousands of books and two families of rats, Beulah Beauford and her husband owned her house. When we moved from apartments in West Jackson to our little house in the Queens, and eventually to North Jackson, I wanted people who dropped me off to think Beulah Beauford's house belonged to us. Our house had more books than any other house I'd ever been in, way more books than Beulah Beauford's house, but no one I knew, other than you, wanted to swim in, or eat, books.

Before dropping me off, you told me I was supposed to use Beulah Beauford's encyclopedias to write a report about these two politicians named Benjamin Franklin Wade and Thaddeus Stevens. You told me to compare their ideas of citizenship to President Ronald Reagan's claim: "We must reject the idea that every time a law's broken, society is guilty rather than the lawbreaker. It is time to restore the American precept that each individual is accountable for his actions."

Then I was also supposed to read the first chapter of William Faulkner's *Absalom, Absalom!* and imitate Faulkner's style when writing a short story placed in Jackson. The first sentence in the book was a million words long, which was cool, and it used strange words like "wisteria" and "lattices," but I didn't know how to write like Faulkner and say anything honest about us. Ronald Reagan gave me the bubble-guts and William Faulkner made me feel drunker than a white man, so I decided I'd take the whupping from you or write lines when I got home.

Besides Layla, and Beulah Beauford's son, Dougie, usually there were at least two other seventeen-year-old big boys in the house who were the friends of Dougie's older cousin, Daryl. Daryl moved into Beulah Beauford's house a year earlier from Minnesota and his room was a straight-up shrine to Vanity, Apollonia, and Prince Rogers Nelson. Daryl and his boys went from rolling their own cigarettes, to smoking weed, to selling tiny things that made people in North Jackson feel better about being alive. In between doing all that smoking and selling, they swam, watched porn, drank Nehis, boiled Red Hots, ate spinach, got drunk, got high, imitated Mike Tyson's voice, talked about running trains, and changed the rules to swim at Beulah Beauford's house every other week that summer of 1987.

One week, the rule was Dougie, Layla, and I had to make

the older boys all the supersweet Kool-Aid they could drink with perfectly chipped ice if we wanted to swim. Two weeks later, the rule was Dougie and I had to place five socks around our fists and box each other until one of our noses bled. The next-to-last day I spent at Beulah Beauford's house, the rule was simple: Layla had to go in Daryl's room with all the big boys for fifteen minutes if she wanted to float in the deep end, and Dougie and I had to steal all the money out of her purse and give it to the big boys when they got out.

Layla, who smelled like apple Now and Laters, shea butter, and bleach, always wore a wrinkled sky-blue swimsuit underneath her acid-washed Guess overalls. I watched her walk down the hall behind Darryl, Wedge, and this dude named Delaney with the biggest calves in the neighborhood. Delaney claimed he'd been initiated into the Vice Lords one weekend earlier.

We all believed him.

When the door to Darryl's bedroom closed, Dougie and I started rummaging through Layla's purse. Stealing stuff, getting to the last level in Donkey Kong, barely losing fights, and saying "on hard," "on punishment," and "on swole" were Dougie's superpowers. He wasn't all-world at any of them, but he did all four ten times more than anyone I'd ever known in Jackson.

Since Layla didn't have any money to steal, Dougie stole Layla's compact that day. He claimed he was going to fill it with these weak joints Daryl showed him how to roll. I saw and stole a crumpled minipack of apple Now and Laters right next to this unopened bottle of white shoe polish.

Inside the smallest pocket of the purse, wrapped around some yellow legal pad paper, was this homemade ID. None of the edges were smooth and Layla had on a red Panama Jack shirt and braces on her bottom teeth in the picture. The ID had Layla's birth date, school name, weight, height, and a church picture of her and her family standing in front of Mt. Calvary, but it didn't have her name on it. I remember Layla was at least six inches shorter and fifty pounds lighter than me. On the other side of the ID, blazing across the middle in huge bleeding black marker, were the words USE THIS IN CASE OF EMERGENCIES.

Up until that point, I'd never really imagined Layla being in one emergency, much less emergencies. Part of it was Layla was a black girl and I was taught by big boys who were taught by big boys who were taught by big boys that black girls would be okay no matter what we did to them. Part of it was Layla was three whole years older than me and I never really had a conversation with her for more than eight seconds. Layla wasn't the most stylish girl in North Jackson, but she was definitely the funniest person in Beulah Beauford's house, and she was all-world at more things than all of us combined. She was all-world at dissing Daryl for having feet that stank through his bootleg Jordans, all-world at reminding Delaney his breaststroke was forever a "drownstroke," and all-world at never really laughing at anyone else's sentences until she was good and ready. I wasn't the type of fat black boy to ever talk to fine black girls first, and Layla wasn't the type of fine black girl to ever really talk to fat black boys like me unless she was asking me to get out of her way, walk faster, or get her some Kool-Aid.

I didn't have an ID of my own, but I did have this blue velcro Jackson State University wallet with the faded tiger on the front. You gave it to me for Christmas. I kept the two-dollar bill Grandmama gave me for my birthday in it. Behind a black-and-white picture of Grandmama, in one of the folds, was one of your old licenses. You said I couldn't leave the house without it until I got my own license. A real license, you told me way more than once, didn't mean I was grown. It just meant I was technically protected from the Vice Lords, the Folks, and the Jackson police, who you claimed worked for Ronald Reagan and the devil.

"What they up in there doing?" I asked Dougie, whose ear was pressed against Daryl's door.

"Fool, what you think? Running a train."

I smirked like I knew what running a train was. Really I had no idea how running a train worked physically or verbally. Running a train sat orange-red in my imagination. Running a train occupied the space of a proper noun, but moved like the most active of active verbs. Just saying "running a train," whether you were a participant in the train or knowledgeable of a train, gave you a glow and gravity every black boy in Jackson respected. The only other three words that gave you a similar glow and gravity were "I got initiated."

"They ran a train up in there this morning, too," Dougie said.

"Layla was here this morning?"

"Naw. It was this other girl."

"Who?"

"I forgot her name," Dougie told me. "LaWon or LaDon some shit. They ran a train on her twice. Be quiet, fool. Listen."

I stood there wondering why the shallow grunts and minisqueaks coming from the boys in Daryl's room made me want to be dead. I didn't know, but I assumed some kind of sex was happening, but I couldn't understand why Layla was so much less breathy than the white women on Cinemax and *The Young and the Restless*. I assumed Layla's short fingers were balled up and her eyes were rolling back in her head. If everyone in the room was naked, I wondered what they all were doing with their hands and how they looked at the hair on each other's thighs. I wondered if anyone was crying.

Fifteen minutes later, the door to the bedroom opened. "Both of y'all little niggas getting on hard, ain't you?" Delaney asked us. Daryl and Wedge walked out of the bedroom a few seconds later with their shirts wrapped around their heads like turbans. Dougie started walking into Daryl's bedroom.

"Where you think you going?" Daryl asked Dougie. "Keece knocked you out like a little-ass trick the other day. Keece, take your big football-playing ass in there and get you some if you want. I think she like you anyway."

I looked at Dougie, who was looking at the ground. "I'm good," I told Daryl, and walked behind the big boys. "I don't want none right now."

When I saw no one was in the bathroom, I acted like I had to pee. After hearing one of the doors to outside close, I walked back down the hallway and stood in the doorway of Daryl's bedroom.

"Big Keece," Layla said from the bedroom. "I be seeing you."

I wasn't sure what Layla saw, other than a twelve-year-old, 213-pound black boy with a suspect hairline and no waves, but under the three crooked Vanity 6 posters and the chlorinated stank of Daryl's bedroom, I saw Layla's Filas were on, and the long stretch marks streaking across the backs of her thighs were so much prettier than the squiggly ones forming on my biceps and butt.

"Big Keece," she said again. "Can you get me some yellow Kool-Aid?"

"Okay," I said. "Wait. Can you tell me how you get your Filas so white?"

"Why you whispering?"

"Oh," I said louder. "I was just wondering how you got your Filas so white."

"Bleach and shoe polish," she said, adjusting the fitted sheet.

"Bleach and shoe polish?"

"Yup. Use bleach first on the white part with, like, a tooth-brush. How come you always be reading books when you come over here?"

"Oh. 'Cause my mama will beat my ass if I don't."

"That's funny," Layla said, and laughed and laughed and laughed until she didn't. "My mama kinda does not play. But I heard your mama *really* does not play."

"She don't," I said, and walked to the kitchen hunting for strawberry Pop-Tarts. I remember watching the swirling reds, yellows, and forest greens in Beulah Beauford's pantry. At our house, there was no pantry. There was hardly any food other than spoiled pimento cheese, the backs of molded wheat bread, a half-empty box of wine, and swollen green olives. I missed our fridge, though. I missed our kitchen.

I missed you.

I opened an unopened bottle of thick bleu cheese dressing and drank as much as I could. Then I placed some crushed ice in a huge red plastic cup, poured some lemonade mix in it. I used a plastic butter knife to stir before walking back to Daryl's bedroom.

From outside the doorway, I could see Layla sitting up,

putting on her swimsuit. I'd only been this close to three naked women in my life: you, Grandmama, and Renata.

"You got me something to drink, Big Keece?"

"I got you some lemonade like you asked me to," I said, still not fully in the room. "And a strawberry Pop-Tart if you want half."

"I want half."

I'd never kissed anyone my age and I worried if Layla tried to kiss me, my lips would be chappy, or my breath would stink like bleu cheese, or at some point she'd maybe see my stretch marks and the big flat mole on my left butt cheek.

I took Layla's ID out of my pocket, grabbed the apple Now and Laters out of my other pocket, put both on the ground to the left of the door. Then I moved the cup of Kool-Aid and the strawberry Pop-Tarts on top of the ID.

"Walk with me out to the pool?" she asked me. "I don't want to go out there by myself."

"Why? You think Daryl and them trying to laugh at you?"

Layla held the strap on her left shoulder and looked down at the Kool-Aid. "I don't," I remember her saying. "I don't think they'll laugh at me. They said I had to go in the bedroom if I wanted to swim in the deep end. So that's what I did."

"Oh," I said. "Yeah."

"Do you?"

"Do I what?"

"Do you think they gone laugh at me?"

"I guess so," I said. "I mean, they be laughing when they nervous. Why you call it yellow Kool-Aid and not lemonade?"

"'Cause that's what it is to me," she said. "It's yellow and it's Kool-Aid. Ain't no lemons in it. Walk out there with me?"

I remember my back facing the opposite side of Daryl's room and wondering if there was a real word for stories filled with people who started off happy and then got sad. "Happysad," no space and no hyphen, was the word I used in my head. Telling happysad stories about what just happened was really all the big boys at Beulah Beauford's house did well. Whether they were true or not didn't matter. What mattered was if they were good stories. Good stories sounded honest. Good stories made you feel like you didn't see all of what you thought you just saw. I knew the big boys would tell stories about what happened in Daryl's bedroom that were good for all three of them and sad for her in three vastly different ways. I wanted to tell Layla some of the happysad stories of our bedrooms but I wasn't sure whether to begin those happysad stories with "I" or "She" or "He" or "We" or "One time" or "Don't tell nobody" or "This might sound nasty to you but . . ."

"I'm starting not to feel so good," I heard Layla say behind me.

"What's wrong?"

"I don't know."

Without turning around, I whispered, "Me either. I mean, me too." Then I took off out of Beulah Beauford's house, leaving Layla to walk by herself toward the deep end.

The run home was a little more than a mile. I ran a lot of sprints in basketball and football practice, and I always felt fast for my size, but I'd never run a mile nonstop. Running a mile for heavy kids like me had everything to do with your brain and your heart forgetting you were running a mile. That's what Dougie, Layla, and me loved about the deep end. For however long you were in it, for a few minutes of your life, no matter how the big boys laughed at us, our bodies forgot how much they weighed.

Then they remembered.

When you and I lived in apartments off Robinson Road, your student Renata came over to babysit a few times a week. Renata, who was bowlegged in one leg, always made pork chops, rice, and gravy. We watched Mid-South Wrestling Saturday night. After Mid-South Wrestling, Renata asked me to come to your bedroom so she could put me in the figure four. While I was on my back bracing myself for pain, Renata told me she loved how my cutoff sweatpants made my thighs and calves look. No one ever said they liked my calves or my thighs before Renata.

When Renata asked if I wanted a sip of her thick Tang, I tried to drink from a part of the cup she hadn't drank from because you told me never to drink after anyone. When Renata asked me why I didn't want to drink after her, I told her because you told me I could get herpes drinking after randoms with chappy lips. "Your mama is the smartest and funniest person I'll ever know," she told me.

"That's cool," I said, and placed my lips right where she pointed. The Tang tasted sweeter than a melted Popsicle and way more sour than a pickle.

"It's good, right?" she asked. "Does it make you want to kiss me?"

I didn't know how to be anything other than scared at the thought I was about to have my first real girlfriend. I remember just fake smiling and drinking more Tang so I could have something to do with my hands.

When I was done with the Tang, Renata pulled up her

shirt, unhooked her bra, and filled my mouth with her left breast. She used her right hand to pinch my nostrils until I could only breathe out of the corners of my mouth.

I held my mouth open as wide as I could, hoping not to cut Renata's breast with my crooked front teeth. I remember praying to God the Tang overpowered the pork chop, rice, and gravy smell on my breath. I didn't think Renata would want to stay my girlfriend if I made one of her nipples smell like pork chops, rice, and gravy. Choking on Renata's breasts made me feel lighter than I'd ever felt. After a few minutes, Renata grabbed my penis and kept saying, "Keep it straight, Kie. Can you keep it straight?" She kept breathing in a way that sounded like she loved whatever her body was feeling. The sound of her breathing made me feel sexy for the second time in my life.

Nearly every time Renata came over to take care of me, she put me in a figure four, choked me, and asked me to keep it straight. When she came over and didn't choke me or ask me to keep it straight, I wondered what was wrong with me. I always assumed it was because my thighs and calves weren't muscly enough. On those days when she didn't touch me, I didn't eat or drink and I did calf raises and squats in the bathroom until I cramped.

After a few months, Renata's real boyfriend came over while she babysat. They drank thick Tang together. Once, when they thought I was asleep, I heard her wailing in the closet and making the same sounds she made with me.

I heard Renata's real boyfriend say, "You better not say no either." Then I heard Renata start cussing him out. I opened the closet door and saw them both standing up, sweaty and naked. Her real boyfriend had the body of Apollo Creed but his neck was longer. I'd never seen Renata's whole naked body that close up. I felt amazed someone with a fine body like hers and a real boyfriend who had a fine body like Apollo Creed would want anything to do with a wide messy body like mine. "Close the closet, little fat, looking-ass nigga," her real boyfriend told me. "Fuck is you looking at?"

When I told them I was going to get your gun to shoot them in the foreheads, they both ran out of the house with half of their clothes on. Renata decided not to be my girlfriend anymore. I never saw her again. I knew it was because my legs were fat and I made her breasts smell like pork chops, rice, and gravy the first time she pushed them in my mouth. You got mad at me that night because your bed looked like two people had been in it. I told you I wasn't in the bed with Renata. I didn't tell you I wanted to be.

The day I sprinted away from Beulah Beauford's house, I sat out in the driveway of our house for hours thinking about what I heard outside of Daryl's bedroom and what I felt in our bedroom. You made me read more books and write more words in response to those books than any of my friends' parents, but nothing I'd ever read prepared me to write or talk about my memory of sex, sound, space, violence, and fear.

Usually, when I wanted to run from memory, I transcribed rap lyrics, or I drew two-story houses, or I wrote poems to Layla, or I watched black sitcoms, or I thought about new ways to act a fool in class, or I shot midrange jump shots, or I ate and drank everything that wasn't nailed down. I couldn't do any of what I wanted to do in our driveway, waiting for you to come home.

When you got home the evening I left Beulah Beauford's house I hugged you, thanked you, told you I loved you. I hated, for the first time, how soft my body felt close to yours. I knew I'd either get a whupping or have to write lines for not doing the assignment you told me to do. Lines were a number of long repeated written sentences explaining what I would do differently, beginning with "I will . . ." I hated writing lines, and always wrote one fewer half line than I was assigned, but I hated getting beaten by you even more.

You turned the lights on when we got in the house and stood in front of one of the bookcases. "What do you see, Kie?" you asked me.

I looked first at your oversized blue dashiki, your wide feet squeezed into a pair of Beulah Beauford's shoes, the shiny keloid on your forearm, and your mini fro leaning slightly left.

"Not *on* me, Kie," you said. "What do you see *behind* me?"

When I was thinking of how to answer your question, you told me you were getting closer to defending your dissertation up in Wisconsin. I hugged your neck, told you how proud I was of you, and asked if that meant you were about to be a real doctor and if being a real doctor meant you'd be making a lot more money.

"Look," you said, and pointed to the bottom shelves of the bookcase. Sitting behind you were the bluest books I'd ever seen. I asked you how we were going to pay for the books since we didn't have enough money for lights or rent. "Kiese Laymon, do you like the encyclopedias or not?"

I stood up and ran my hands along the spines. You usually only said my whole name when I was about to get a whupping. "Does this mean I don't have to go to Beulah Beauford's house no more?"

"Smell the books," you said, and opened the encyclopedia on the far left. "Get a grip. And don't say 'no more.' Say anymore."

"Anymore," I said, and put my nose as close as I could to the spine of the book. You told me my first assignment was to use our encyclopedias to write a two-page report on Jim Crow and freedom strategies used by black elected officials in Mississippi, post-Reconstruction. The report was due by the end of the week.

"Um," I told you before you walked to your room to call Malachi Hunter, "I think I want to lose weight. Can you help me? I be sweating too much when I try to talk to people I don't want to be sweaty around."

"You mean girls, Kie?"

"I guess I mean girls."

"If someone doesn't like you for you," you said, "they are not worth sweating around. Save your sweat for someone who values it. I think I'm gaining all the weight you want to lose in my thighs."

Your thighs were always thick, but I could see even less of your cheekbones in the last few months. Your neck looked a lot shorter. Your breasts seemed heavier when you walked around the house in your huge raggedy Jackson State T-shirt. You looked even more beautiful to me.

We played Scrabble that evening and I beat you for the second time in our lives. You asked for a rematch, and I beat you again. "I'm surprised you didn't try to spell 'be' or 'finna' every chance you got," you said as you walked toward our new encyclopedias. I watched you stand in front of the encyclopedias with your sweatpants and JSU T-shirt on. You smiled ear to ear as you gently fingered through half of the books. "The day your grandmother brought home a set of encyclopedias for us was the happiest day of my childhood, Kie."

"Do I have to go to Beulah Beauford's house anymore to use her encyclopedias if we have our own?"

You responded to my question with a question, which is something you said was illegal in our house, and asked if I used Beulah Beauford's encyclopedias to write the essay or short story you told me to write. "If you didn't write the essay or the story, what did you do?" You actually stood there, with an encyclopedia in hand, waiting for an answer. "Answer me, Kie. Don't tell a story either."

I thought about what I did, what I wrote, what I saw and heard, and how I ran away. I imagined Layla telling a story of that day. I could hear her telling it in a style that made me better than the big boys. I could hear her telling it in a style that made me worse. I could mostly hear her telling it in a style that centered her and made the big boys, Dougie, and me the same kind of blurry and terrible.

When I didn't answer your question, you said my not doing the essay was another tired example of refusing to strive for excellence, education, and accountability when excellence, education, and accountability were requirements for keeping the insides of black boys in Mississippi healthy and safe from white folk.

I stood there watching you, feeling a lot about what it meant to be a healthy, safe black boy in Mississippi, and wondering why folk never talked about what was needed to keep black girls healthy and safe. My body knew things my mouth and my mind couldn't, or maybe wouldn't, express. It knew that all over my neighborhood, boys were trained to harm girls in ways girls could never harm boys, straight kids were trained to harm queer kids in ways queer kids could never harm straight kids, men were trained to harm women in ways women could never harm men, parents were trained to harm children in ways children would never harm parents, babysitters were trained to harm kids in ways kids could never harm babysitters. My body knew white folk were trained to harm us in ways we could never harm them. I didn't know how to tell you or anyone else the stories my body told me, but, like you, I knew how to run, deflect, and duck.

"Kiese Laymon, what did you do instead of writing your essay?" you asked me again. "I am going to ask you one more time and I am going to get my belt. Why did you not do the work I told you to do?"

I wanted to tell you I hated when you didn't use contractions. Instead I said, "I'm sorry. I just got tired of swimming in the deep end at Beulah Beauford's house, and I wanted to come home. I won't do it again. Thank you for the new encyclopedias. I know they gone protect my insides from white folk."

"Going to," you said. "Don't say 'gone' or 'gonna,' Kie. 'They are going to protect your insides.' If you know better, do better. Promise me you will do better."

"Now?"

"Yes, now. Do you promise?"

"Yes."

"Say it."

"I promise," I said. "I promise."

You didn't beat me. You made me write ten lines instead. I wrote nine and a half because I was hardheaded.

I promise to read and write as I'm told when I go to Beulah Beauford's house.

I promise to read and write as I'm told when I go to Beulah Beauford's house.

I promise to read and write as I'm told when I go to Beulah Beauford's house.

I promise to read and write as I'm told when I go to Beulah Beauford's house.

I promise to read and write as I'm told when I go to Beulah Beauford's house.

I promise to read and write as I'm told when I go to Beulah Beauford's house.

I promise to read and write as I'm told when I go to Beulah Beauford's house.

I promise to read and write as I'm told when I go to Beulah Beauford's house.

I promise to read and write as I'm told when I go to Beulah Beauford's house.

I promise to read and write as I'm told.

NAN

Later that night, at Jitney Jungle, you filled our cart with cream of mushroom soup, tuna, name-brand wheat bread, and a big bottle of off-brand cranberry juice. I asked you if I could get the latest issue of *Right On!* magazine because Salt-N-Pepa were on the cover. You told me to just read it while we waited in line. When we walked up to the checkout, I put all the food on the conveyor belt and watched it glide away from us. Behind the cashier, pinned to a board, were a number of checks and Xeroxes of licenses, with the words DO NOT ACCEPT NAN CHECK FROM THESE CUSTOMERS in all caps. A Xerox of your license and one of your checks from Trustmark was in the middle of the board. Your check looked like the undisputed champion of bounced checks at Jitney Jungle.

"Let's go," I said as I watched you go in your purse and pull out your checkbook. "I ain't even hungry."

"Kie, do not say 'ain't.'"

"Okay. I won't say 'ain't' again," I told you. "Can we just go?"

You looked in the direction of the older black woman cashier. She looked like a black version of Vera from the TV show *Alice*, but she had thicker lips and smaller teeth. "These folk don't even know when to use 'nan' or when to use 'any,'" you said. I wasn't sure if you saw your picture or not, but I watched your shoulders dip as air left your chest. "You're

30

right, Kie," you said. "Let's just go. There's tuna and crackers at home."

I told you I thought the person who wrote the sign, just like Grandmama, used "nan" to mean "not any" or "not one."

"Don't excuse mediocrity," you told me.

"So Grandmama is mediocre?"

"Grandmama had to work for white folk instead of going to high school, and she finished high school through correspondence classes. She has an excuse to use the language she uses. What are these people's excuse?"

"I don't know. We don't even know them."

"Don't excuse mediocrity, Kie," you told me again as we walked out of the store hand in hand. You looked toward the sky. "I hope Grandmama is out on her porch looking at the stars tonight. The sky is so clear."

Every now and then, Grandmama sent these Mason jars of pickles and pear preserves. Or she gave us pounds of government cheese, peanut butter, and crackers near the middle of the month. Grandmama laughed and laughed until she didn't when I called the cheese Gourmet African American cheese. You tried to act too good to eat Gourmet African American cheese, but sometimes I caught you making these buttery grilled Gourmet African American cheese sandwiches with something ultrabougie like pumpernickel bread. I couldn't understand why you were so ashamed of eating like we didn't have much money, so ashamed of demanding my father pay his child support.

On the walk to the car, I wondered what it felt like to have a face like yours, one of the most beautiful recognizable faces in our world, plastered on the wall at the biggest grocery store in North Jackson because you claimed you had money in the bank you didn't really have. You were the only local black political scientist on TV during election season talking about politics. The way you overpronounced your words, defended poor black communities in the face of white resentment, and insisted on correcting everyone whose subjects and verbs didn't agree made black folk in Jackson think we had plenty of lunch money, gas money, rent money, and light bill money.

We didn't.

"Why'd they put a picture of your license up there, like you robbed a bank?" I asked you in the parking lot. "Can you tell me?"

"I'm just tired, Kie," you said. "You know how hard Grandmama had to fight to get line work in that chicken plant?"

"I think I do," I told you. "Want me to drive?"

We were two miles from the house and you weren't making a drop of sense. You talked like this a few years earlier before collapsing.

"I'm just so tired," you kept saying, now from the passenger seat. "I work hard, Kie. I really do. I work so hard. They never pay us what we're worth. I try to tell Mama the same thing. Drive slowly, Kie." I reached over and held the warm fold underneath the curve of your knee. That's what you did for me when I was sad.

By the time we made it home, you were snoring. I didn't want to wake you so I turned off the Nova in the driveway and pushed the driver's seat back. I sat there watching you breathe with your chin tucked into your left shoulder.

I watched you sleep and thought about how a few weeks earlier, you had this party for your students at the house. You played a mix of Anita Baker, Sade, Patrice Rushen, and Phil Collins all night long. Malachi Hunter was there but he didn't do much other than drink bourbon and watch you. The house was filled with students who'd fallen in love with you. Shareece wanted to watch you laugh. Cornell wanted to watch you dance. Carlton wanted to watch you talk. Judy wanted to watch you listen.

Near the end of the night, you sat at a table with Beulah Beauford. You said something about how "infinitely finer" Denzel was than Bryant Gumbel or Dr. J, and everyone around the table burst out laughing. I watched you look up at Malachi Hunter, who was grinning ear to ear in the kitchen. Malachi Hunter knew, whether he deserved it or not, he'd been chosen by the freshest woman in our world.

Sitting in the Nova, I took out my wallet, got your old license, and placed it on the dashboard. That summer day, the day Dougie said "running a train," the day I left Layla alone at Beulah Beauford's house, the day I slipped around the memory of what happened with Renata in our bedroom, the day you bought new encyclopedias intended to save my insides from white folk, you and I held on to each other like we were the first people in the world to float over, under, and around all the orange-red stars in the galaxy.

I might have liked the raggedy psychologist you got Hunter Malachi to pay for me to see two days later if she hadn't tried so hard to talk proper, and ask me all these questions about parents, food, and church, or if you didn't sit in the same room with us the whole time. The first question the psychologist asked was how I felt about my parents getting divorced.

"I don't think about it much," I told her.

She asked me to tell her everything I remembered about my parents being together. I told her how y'all met as sophomores

33

and juniors at Jackson State University in 1973. I told her that ten months after y'all met, you were pregnant with me. My father was in Zaire during the entire pregnancy. You weren't alone during the thirty-two-hour labor and C-section though. Grandmama was there. My father sent the name "Kiese" to you in a letter a few weeks before my birth. You told him you wanted my first name to be "Citoyen" and my middle name to be "Makeba," after Miriam Makeba, the South African singer and freedom fighter.

The psychologist thought I was lying when I told her I had no Mississippi memories of my father. I told her pictures showed me my father was in Mississippi with us. Pictures said he loved tight short shorts, and red, black, and green knit hats, and he appreciated pondering tough questions and getting high under the gritting teeth and pointed finger of Malcolm X. I told her my first memories of my father came after y'all stopped seeing each other in Madison. When you dropped me off one Saturday, you gave me some money Grandmama sent us. I was supposed to give my father the money so he could afford groceries. I didn't remember how much it was, but I took a dollar of it and put it in my pocket before I handed it to him. It just didn't make sense to me that we had no food in our fridge, yet here we were giving my father money Grandmama had given us.

Life at my father's Wisconsin apartment was different from our life. I remember both places having lots of music and incense, but there were so many rules at my father's apartment. People had to take their shoes off when they came in. I couldn't ever put my hands on the walls. One time I went to do laundry with him at the laundromat and he saw some skid marks in my underwear. He swore it was because you weren't teaching me how to wipe my ass correctly. When I wiped my ass in his apartment, I couldn't use more than four pieces of toilet paper. And the toilet paper had to be folded perfectly, not balled up. When we ate, my father had every bit of food planned out. And there was always lots of space between whatever he put on my plate.

"Presentation matters," I remember him saying. "So do patience and discipline. Take your time eating, son."

That day, my father brought out these snowballs he'd frozen from the winter so we could have a snowball fight in the summer. After the snowball fight, we walked down to the dumpster near our apartment complex, where we saw this baby raccoon. I'd never seen the baby of a raccoon, or possum, up close. I was so afraid, not just to touch it but to even witness it trying to live. My father picked me up and let me peek down deeper in the dumpster. The baby raccoon messed around in some trash with its crazy-short arms, then it looked up at us and I jerked my body back as fast as I could.

I remember folding up my arms, sticking out my lips, and just looking at my father while he was dying laughing. It was the first time I'd ever seen him just be a normal goofy person. After a while, I followed my father behind the dumpster to Lake Mendota, where I watched him throw rocks at the sun that never came down.

That's what I told the psychologist about my memories of my father. For some reason, it made you cry.

"Might you talk to me a bit more about violence?" the psychologist asked me after my story.

I looked over at you. You were cross-legged, looking at me misty-eyed. "What do you mean?" I asked her.

"What I mean is this: if you're having problems with violence at school, I wonder how you're experiencing violence at home."

"I ain't having problems with violence at school," I said. "I ain't having problems with violence at home either."

The psychologist told me you said I had a violence problem. I wondered when you met with her and why I couldn't have been there to just watch you talk like you were watching me. "Your mother contends you eat and drink things you shouldn't be eating or drinking when you're angry. She said you have turned to alcohol. I want you to tell me about your experiences with alcohol and violence at home or at school."

I looked over at you again. "I drank Mason jars of box wine three times when there wasn't nothing else to eat or drink because it's sweeter than water."

"Count to ten," the psychologist abruptly told me.

"What you mean?"

"It's clear you're harboring anger over your parents' separating and I think counting might help. Use this technique when you feel yourself getting angry about the divorce no matter where you are, or when you feel yourself wanting to drink wine, or eat sugary foods, go to the bathroom and count to ten."

"Is a technique like a style?"

"Yes."

"But I don't feel nan amount of anger at all about them not being together," I told her. "I mean, I got my grandmama, too. I don't feel nan amount of anger at all over them being divorced. I be wishing my father paid child support more, but I'm good."

"Don't say 'be,' " you said from across the room. "Don't say 'nan' either. He's just showing out right now."

36

"I wish my father paid his child support on time," I said. "But I'm good."

"Do me a favor," the psychologist said as she walked us to the door. "Remember, in case of an emergency, I'd like for both of you to find a quiet space away from each other and just count to ten. If it's dark, go outside and count at least ten stars. Everything that seems wrong might seem right if you just do this exercise. I think it might also help if you both limit your sugar and carbs and get more physical exercise."

When we got home, you and I played our last game of one-on-one in the driveway. Your student Carlton Reeves put a goal in our front yard a year earlier and we'd played 21 a few times a month since then. When we first played, I was scared of how physical you were on offense and defense. I was taller than you, heavier than you, more skilled than you, stronger than you, but it didn't matter. On offense, when you didn't shoot your high arching one-handed jumpshot from your right hip, you backed me down by lunging your butt into my thighs. When you were close enough to the goal, you either shot a strange hook shot or pump-faked.

That day, though, I was too tall to go for pump-fakes and my calves were too strong to let you back me down. I blocked your first three shots into the azaleas of the family next door. On offense, I just shot over you, or blew by you with a jab step left. That day, though, I realized I could have beaten you a year earlier. And you realized I could have beaten you a year earlier. And neither of us felt happy about that fact. I kept getting to twenty and missing the free throw on purpose so you could get closer.

At some point, we had to decide if I would win. Your neck

was glowing with sweat. I don't know why but beating you felt harmful. I didn't want to hurt your feelings. Knowing, or accepting I could beat you was enough for me. We both knew that game would be the last game we ever played no matter the score because we both knew, without saying it, you needed to not lose much more than I needed to win. When you made the last shot of the game, you celebrated, hugged my neck, told me good game, and held my hand.

"Thank you for letting me win, Kie," you said. "I needed that. And thank you for what you did today at the counselor's office."

I remember looking at you and believing we'd turned a page in our relationship. We were about to limit our sugar and carbs. We were about to exercise more. And no matter what happened next, we would both go outside and count at least ten stars until everything wrong in our world felt right.

WET

"Kie, I'm not going to tell you again," you said the next morning. We were sitting in the Nova in Beulah Beauford's driveway. "Get out of this car." I couldn't tell you why I didn't want to stay at Beulah Beauford's house. You claimed you needed to go do some organizing and research in Sunflower County for Jesse Jackson's presidential campaign and you didn't want me at the house alone because someone broke in a few months earlier. I told you I knew you were lying and I knew you were going to see Hunter Malachi. "Kiese Laymon, I'm not about to tell you again. Get a grip. And get your fat ass out of my car."

I stood outside the Nova with my arms folded, covering my belly and my chest. You'd never called me fat. I didn't think you saw it.

"You better have that essay done when I pick you up, too," you said. "I'm tired of playing with you."

From outside the door, I opened my wallet, got your old license out, and tossed it through the window of the car. You threw the license back out of the passenger window and reversed out of the driveway.

Layla didn't come back to Beulah Beauford's house that Sunday but Daryl, Delaney, and Wedge did. I asked Dougie what happened after I left the house. He said everyone ate hamburgers, drank forties, and smoked weed until more girls came over. He said the girls who came over were older than Layla, and two of them had to go in Daryl's room with all the big boys just like Layla did.

Late that Sunday afternoon, I noticed almost all of us were in the pool except for Dougie. Sometimes when Dougie left, he'd just go make everyone cheeseburgers, but he'd been gone for a while so I got out of the pool, too.

I walked back to Dougie's bedroom. No one was there.

I walked into the bathroom in the hall, but no one was there, either. Down the hall a bit from his room, I saw Daryl's bedroom door cracked.

I got close enough to the door to see Delaney was standing in the middle of the room with his soggy maroon swim trunks around his calves. Dougie was on his knees in front of Delaney with his hands behind his back. His tongue was out, licking the tip of Delaney's penis.

As soon as they saw me, Delaney pulled up his swim trunks. Dougie dusted his hands off on his Pittsburgh Steelers shirt and walked right by me with his head down. I turned, walked down the hall, and got ready to fight or sprint out of Beulah Beauford's front door. Delaney grabbed my arm and asked me to sit down in the living room.

I sat on the stool in front of Beulah Beauford's piano and Delaney sat next to me. He told me he would teach me to play "Chopsticks" if I promised not to tell anyone what I saw.

I sat with both fists balled up on my thighs. Part of me wanted Delaney to touch me again so I could try to kill him. But the biggest part of me was afraid Delaney might make me get on my knees, make me put my hands behind my back, make me lick the head of his penis until he said stop.

I sat there, watching those still piano keys, and half listening to Delaney play and slowly talk his way through how he learned "Chopsticks."

When he was done, Delaney stood up and looked down at me one more time.

"Don't tell nobody, okay?" he said. "I'm serious. I was just playing with that boy. It was just a game. You hear me?"

Grandmama always taught me to empty my pockets before I swung on somebody, so I went in both pockets, took out my wet wallet, and slammed your license down on the piano.

Delaney looked at the ID. "That's your mama? She work with my daddy. Please don't say nothing to your mama. Your mama does not play. My daddy gone fuck me up if he finds out. I'm for real. That's just how me and D be playing. I'm for real."

I followed Delaney out of Beulah Beauford's front door and watched him sprint down the road like he was being chased until his wind got bad. That's when he started walking, looking behind him, and pointing at me like his fingers were guns.

A few seconds later, Delaney was out of sight.

I sat down in Beulah Beauford's rocky driveway and started making thick-lipped smiley faces with the rocks. My head hurt. I didn't understand why Delaney thought teaching me "Chopsticks" would make what he did okay, or why Dougie's hands were behind his back while he was on his knees. I didn't understand why Delaney seemed so happy to be a part of a train but so scared for me to know what he did with Dougie. A part of me didn't understand why the big boys wanted to be in rooms alone with Dougie and Layla and not me. A part of me knew it was because I was the fattest, sweatiest person in Beulah Beauford's house.

Ever since we were old enough to spend the night or day at our friends' houses, we'd all play this game called "Hide and Go Get It." One person had to count to thirty-five and the other people had to hide, usually in a dark closet or hallway. We played with boys and girls, but in the dark of those hallways and closets, sometimes folk would touch each other in ways they'd never touch each other when the lights were on. I was too afraid to touch anyone, but not too afraid to want to be touched. My body didn't care if the person touching me was a boy or girl. My body felt grateful for tender touch no matter where it came from.

Around the same time, girls and girls' bodies and girls' booties and girls' touch made me feel not just special but sexier and more beautiful than boys' touch and boys' booties. I didn't know why and I wasn't sure how to use words to explain it. I didn't know who would listen to me explain something so scary even if I thought I'd found the words. I kept thinking you should have been the one I talked with about it all since you were the one who taught me to read and write. But sexuality and bodies and feeling good and pain and tender touch and booties were something we never ever talked about.

My body told different stories about you and Renata. Even though her touch was rough and yours was gentle, when either of you touched me, it all felt like love until it didn't. Then it felt like dying. Though I had no idea what was going through Layla's and Dougie's heads and bodies as they walked in Daryl's bedroom, I wondered if they ever felt love while they were in there with the big boys.

I know I would have.

Every half an hour, I went back into Beulah Beauford's and

42

called Malachi Hunter's house looking for you. I hated that I could never forget Malachi Hunter's phone number, hated how I could trace the shape of every syllable on his answering machine message.

"You have reached the home of Malachi J. Hunter, the Alpha and Omega of Real Estate Agents in the new South. I am unavailable. Please leave a detailed message and I will return your call. Thank you."

Malachi Hunter's favorite way to start sentences was "That damn white man." According to Malachi Hunter, that damn white man's crowning failure was that he overestimated himself and underestimated the resolve of "the revolutionary black man in Mississippi." There were no black women, white women, or Mexican women in Malachi Hunter's political imagination. But once I understood that Malachi Hunter was "the revolutionary black man in Mississippi" to Malachi Hunter, and being "the revolutionary black man in Mississippi" meant carrying himself like he saw rich radical white men carry themselves in Mississippi, I understood almost everything I needed to know about Malachi Hunter.

You and Malachi Hunter didn't share the same political imaginations about black folk in Mississippi. You were more invested in organizing, teaching, grassroots political movement to help black folk in rural Mississippi exit poverty and shield ourselves from white folk's negligence. Malachi Hunter was much more invested in becoming a black southern symbol of wealth and black power before he was fifty. But when it came to kids, y'all were both invested, and really obsessed with what y'all called "redeeming value." Y'all didn't think black children should watch shows, listen to music, or read

43

books with violence, nudity, adult situations, or cussing because violence, nudity, adult situations, and cussing lacked redeeming value.

I always thought that was funny.

"This Kie," I said into Malachi Hunter's answering machine again. "Please come get me. You told me you would beat me if I went home, so I'm just waiting here in Beulah Beauford driveway. Please come. Beulah Beauford house, it make my head hurt. It's real sad over here."

An hour later, you pulled up. It didn't matter where I was, how late you were, or how angry we were with each other when you dropped me off, nothing on earth felt as good as watching you pull up in our Nova to pick me up.

"I love you," I told you as I got in the Nova. You didn't say anything. "I love you," I said again. Your right cheek was quivering. "You ain't hear me leaving messages?"

"Put your seat belt on," you said in the most brittle voice I'd ever heard come out of your head. You'd just started making me wear my seat belt a week earlier. I put the seat belt on when a round, clear tear slid down your cheek. The tear slowed down, sped up past your thin top lip, and slipped into the black corner of your mouth. I'd seen you cry when you talked to me about my grades, or when you lied about having more money than you did, or when you created some strange lie about why my father didn't send child support.

I put my left hand on the right fist you used to steer our Nova. "How come you can't look at me?" You stopped the Nova at the stop sign on the corner of Beasley and Hanging Moss and slowly turned your face to mine.

The white of your left eye was filled with a cloud of blood. The brown flesh around the eye was darker and puffed up twice its normal size. It looked like someone put a tiny plum under your eyelid.

When we got to the house, you knew what I was going to get. You pushed me away and rushed into your room. I watched you lift your pillow where you kept your gun. If I got to it first, you knew I would use it.

Instead of going to my room, I got ice, napkins, a jar of pear preserves, a spoon, and our butcher knife.

"You gotta be still, for real," I told you, wiping the dried blood off your face with thumbs wet from my saliva.

"Have to be," you said. "Don't say 'gotta.' "

"Gotta," I said. "Gotta. They gotta have fleas at Beulah Beauford's house. The fleas over there, they gotta be the maddest fleas in the world the way they be biting me all upside the head. Gotta."

You laughed so hard and told me not to use the word "be" like that. I hoped you'd never stop laughing. "I don't want any pear preserves, Kie," you told me. "Not now."

"How come?"

"They too sweet."

When you finally put your arm around my neck, I felt all of your weight. "Hold me tight, Kie," you said from our bed. "You're my best friend. I'm sorry," you said as you fell asleep with the covers over the swollen, slick parts of your face. "I'm sorry for all of this."

"You my best friend, too," I told you. "My best friend ever."

Lying next to you in that bed, I remembered the first time you told me I was your best friend. I knew you kissed my cheeks because you loved me. I knew you asked me to hold you tighter because you loved me. You were so gentle. For more than a year, this was how we spent some of our mornings in my room and yours. Then you met Malachi Hunter. A few weeks later, you started to beat me for talking back and for way-less-than-excellent grades. Sometimes you'd beat me upside the head. Sometimes you'd beat me across the hands. Sometimes you'd beat me as hard as you could in my mouth with belts, shoes, fists, and clothes hangers.

I remember you making me take my clothes off and lie across the same bed we used to sleep in. I don't think I've ever screamed like that. You made me put my face down into the bed so I couldn't brace myself. As much as the lashes hurt, knowing you were beating me at nine years old as hard as you could while looking at my fat naked black body hurt way more. The tearing of flesh hurt less than it should have, I think, because I knew you didn't really want to hurt me. I knew you didn't want to hurt me because you sometimes touched me like you loved me. I wish you could have just chosen one kind of touch, even if it was just beating me ten times a day every day.

That would have made everything a lot less confusing.

You were still snoring when Malachi Hunter pulled his black Volvo into our driveway. You woke up when I tried to kill a revolutionary black man from Mississippi for hurting you that night.

Two hours later, you and Malachi Hunter took one glass of wine to your bedroom. From my bed, I heard long-tailed rats hiking through our walls, wet tires skating past our windows, and Johnny Carson's nasal monologue. I couldn't hear your voice, the only voice I wanted to hear when I woke up, the last voice I wanted to hear before going to sleep.

I opened the bedroom door, walked down the hallway a

few feet from your bedroom. Behind a locked door, Malachi Hunter said he was sorry for punching you in your face, sorry for making you bleed, sorry for fighting your son, sorry for punishing you for wanting to know the truth. You told Malachi Hunter you wanted a daughter and you were sorry for running away.

I went back to my room and heard your bedroom door unlock and lock again.

The minisqueaks from your bed got louder. I got on my knees and prayed to God not to hear you wailing under the weight of the revolutionary black man from Mississippi.

I hated my body.

I walked in the kitchen, got the biggest spoon I could find, and dipped it halfway in the peanut butter and pear preserves Grandmama had given us. I heard the wailing all the way in the kitchen. I dipped the same spoon a quarter deep into Grandmama's pear preserves and put the whole spoon in my mouth. I did it again and again until the jar of peanut butter was gone.

The wailing didn't stop. I hated my body.

Before leaving the kitchen, I gulped down a few Mason jars of box wine until I forgot the shape of the sound I was running from. When I was supposed to be finishing my report for you on Fannie Lou Hamer, I wrote instead about losing my twelve-year-old heavy black body to an emergency I was too sad, too drunk—and really too terrified—to identify.

Early the next morning, I had my first wet dream. I was afraid to tell you what my body did while you were with Malachi Hunter because I knew you'd ask me why. Though I never wanted you to touch me again, I didn't want to lie to you. Lying to you felt like cheating. Cheating felt like something I never wanted to do to my best friend.

BE

A few weeks into the summer, when counting to ten and limiting sugar and simple carbohydrates didn't work for either of us, you dropped me off with Grandmama for a few days in Forest, Mississippi. I loved Grandmama but I didn't really love going to her house any day other than Friday. Every Friday, Grandmama let me watch *Dukes of Hazzard*, a show you said "operates in a world even more racist than the one we live in, where two white drug dealers who keep violating probation and making fools of the police in a red Dodge Charger with the Confederate flag on top called the *General Lee* never go to prison."

The Friday night I was sent to stay with Grandmama, I asked her if black folk like us could ever get away from the police like Bo and Luke Duke could.

"No," Grandmama said before I could get the whole question out. "Nope. Not at all. Never. You better never try that mess either, Kie."

The one or two times there were black characters on *Dukes of Hazzard*, I remember Grandmama and her boyfriend, Ofa D, getting closer to the screen and cheering for them the same way they cheered if the Georgetown Hoyas were playing, if Jackson State won, or if there was a black contestant on *Wheel of Fortune*.

Like most black women in Forest, Grandmama had a

number of side hustles in addition to working the line at the chicken plant. One of her side hustles was selling vegetables from her garden. Another side hustle was selling fried fish, pound cakes, and sweet potato pies every Saturday evening to anyone who would buy them. The most important of Grandmama's side hustles was washing clothes, ironing, cooking, and doing dishes for this white family called the Mumfords.

After church, that Sunday, on the way to the Mumfords, I complained to Grandmama my slacks were so tight I had to unzip them to breathe. Grandmama laughed and laughed and laughed until she didn't. She said she wouldn't be at the Mumfords for long. I always saw the Mumfords' nasty clothes next to Grandmama's washer, and their clean clothes out on the clothesline behind her house.

I hated those clothes.

The Mumfords lived right off Highway 35. I was amazed at how the houses off Highway 35 were the only houses in Forest that looked like the houses on *Leave It to Beaver, Who's the Boss?*, and *Mr. Belvedere*. When I imagined the insides of rich-white-folk houses, I imagined stealing all their food while they were asleep. I wanted to gobble up palms full of Crunch 'n Munch and fill up their thirty-two-ounce glasses with name-brand ginger ale and crushed ice tumbling out of their silver refrigerators. I wanted to leave the empty glasses and Crunch 'n Munch crumbs on the counter so the white folk would know I'd been there and they'd have something to clean up when I left.

Grandmama left the key in the ignition and told me she'd be back in about twenty minutes. "Don't say nothing to that badass Mumford boy if he come out here, Kie," she said. "He ain't got a lick of home training. You hear me? Don't get out of this car unless it's an emergency."

I nodded yes and sprawled out across the front seat of the Impala. Damn near as soon as Grandmama went in the house, out came this boy who looked like a nine-year-old Mike D from the Beastie Boys. The Mumford boy was bone-white and skinny in a way Grandmama called "po'." Grandmama didn't have much money, and her six-hundred-square-foot shotgun house was clean as Clorox on the inside, but raggedy as a roach on the outside. I always wondered why Grandmama never called people with less stuff than us "po'." She called them "folk who ain't got a pot to piss in" or "folk whose money ain't all the way right" or "folk with nan dime to they name" but she never used "poor" or "po'" to talk about anything other than people's bodies.

Without knocking, the po' white boy opened the door of the driver's side of Grandmama's Impala. "You Reno's grandson?" he asked me.

"Who is Reno?"

"You know Reno. The old black lady who clean my house."

I'd never seen this po' white boy before but I'd seen the shiny gray Jams swim trunks, the long two-striped socks and the gray Luke Skywalker shirt he had on in our dirty clothes basket, and hanging on our clothesline. I didn't like how knowing a po' white boy's clothes before knowing a po' white boy made me feel. And I hated how this po' white boy called Grandmama "Reno, the old black lady who clean my house."

I got out of the Impala and kept my hands in my pockets. "So you Reno's grandson?" the boy asked. "You the one from Jackson?"

Before I could say yes, the Mumford boy told me we couldn't come in his house but we could play in the backyard. The phrase "I'm good" was something I always said in Jackson, but I didn't know I had ever meant it as much as I meant it that day.

That's what I felt before I looked at the size of the Mumfords' garage and saw a closet door open in the left corner. I walked toward the room and saw a washer, a dryer, and a scale on the ground.

"What y'all call this room?" I asked him.

"That's our washroom," he said. "Why y'all stay shooting folk in Jackson? Can I ask you that?"

I ignored the po' white boy's question. At Grandmama's house, our washer was in the dining room and we didn't have a dryer, so we hung everything up on the clothesline. "Wait. What's a scale doing in there?"

"My pawpaw like to weigh himself out here."

"That washer, do it work?"

"It work fine," he said. "Good as new."

"And the dryer, too?" I looked at the two irons on this shelf hanging above a new ironing board. I didn't know how to say what I wanted to say. I stepped on the scale in the corner. "This scale, it's right?"

"Don't ask me," he said. "I never used it. I told you it's my pawpaw scale."

I walked back to Grandmama's Impala, got in the driver's seat, and locked the doors. I remember gripping the steering wheel with one hand and digging my fingernails into my knee with the other hand. I wondered how fat 218 pounds really was for twelve years old.

Less than a minute after I was in the car, the Mumford boy

came back out. Without knocking, he tried to open the Impala's driver-side door again.

"Come on in and play, Jackson," he said again from outside the car.

"Naw. I'm good," I told him, and rolled the window down.

"You wanna shoot squirrels in the head with my pellet gun in the backyard?"

"Naw," I told him. "My mama don't let me shoot squirrels in the head. I'm not allowed to shoot guns. I'm good."

"But all y'all do is shoot guns in Jackson."

I sat in Grandmama's Impala with a rot spreading in my chest for a few seconds before Grandmama walked out of the house carrying a basket of dirty clothes. An envelope sat on top of the clothes.

When I told Grandmama what the Mumford boy said to me, she told me to leave these folk alone. "Do you know who you messing with?" she asked me. "These white folk, they liable to have us locked up under the jail, Kie."

I kept looking at Grandmama as we drove home. I was trying to decide if I should ask her why she had to wash, dry, iron, and fold the Mumfords' nasty clothes if the Mumfords had a better washer than ours, a working dryer, a newer iron, and an ironing board. I wanted to ask her if there were better side hustles than washing nasty white-folk clothes on the weekend. But I didn't say anything on the first half of the way home. I just looked at Grandmama's face and saw deeper frown lines around her mouth than I'd ever seen before.

I wanted to shrink and slide down Grandmama's frown lines.

I understood that day why you and Grandmama were so hungry for black wins, regardless of how tiny those wins were. For Grandmama, those wins were always personal. For you, the wins were always political. Both of y'all knew, and showed me, how we didn't even have to win for white folk to punish us. All we had to do was not lose the way they wanted us to.

I kept wishing I would have gone in the Mumfords' house and stolen all their food. Stealing their food felt like the only way to make the rotten feeling in my belly go away.

Before going home, Grandmama took the envelope she'd gotten from the Mumfords', wrote your name and address on it, and put it in the mailbox downtown.

"Grandmama," I said, as we turned down Old Morton Road, "do those white folk know your name is Catherine or do they think your name is Reno?"

"I know my name," Grandmama said, "and I know how much these white folk pay me every week."

"Do you tell the Mumfords the truth when you're in their house?"

"Naw," she said. "I shole don't."

"Then what you be telling them?"

"I be telling them whatever it takes to get they little money and take care of my family."

"But do you ever wanna steal they food?"

"Naw, Kie," she said. "They test me like that all the time. If I ever stole from them folk, we wouldn't have nothing. You hear me? Nothing. I'm telling you what I know now. Do not steal nothing from no white folk. Ever. Or you likely to be off in hell with them folk one day."

In Grandmama's world, most white folk were destined for hell, not because they were white, but because they were fake Christians who hadn't really heeded their Bibles. Grandmama

53

really believed only two things could halt white folks' inevitable trek into hell: appropriate doses of Jesus and immediate immersion in Concord Missionary Baptist church. I didn't understand hell, or the devil, but I understood Concord Missionary Baptist church.

And I hated most of it.

My slacks were too tight in Sunday school so they were always flooding. My shirt choked my esophagus. My clip-on tie looked like a clip-on tie. No matter the temperature, Grandmama made me wear a polyester vest. My feet grew so fast that my penny loafers never fit. Plus, she stopped me from putting dimes or nickels in my penny loafers because that was something only mannish boys did.

Inside Concord Missionary Baptist church, I loved the attention I got for being a fat black boy from the older black women: they were the only women on earth who called my fatness fineness. I felt flirted with, and like most fat black boys, when flirted with, I fell in love. I loved the organ's bended notes, the aftertaste of the grape juice, the fans steadily moving through the humidity, the anticipation of somebody catching the Holy Ghost, the lawd-have-mercy claps after the little big-head boy who couldn't read so well was forced to read a greeting to the congregation.

But as much as I loved parts of church, and as hard as I tried, I couldn't love the holy word coming from the pulpit. The voices carrying the word were slick and sure of themselves in ways I didn't believe. The word at Concord was always carried by the mouths of the reverend, deacons, or other visiting preachers who acted like they knew my grandmama and her friends better than they did.

Older black women in the church made up the majority

of the audience. But their voices and words were only heard during songs, in ad-libbed responses to the preacher's word and during church announcements. While Grandmama and everyone else amen'd and well'd their way through shiny hollow sermons, I just sat there, usually at the end of the pew, sucking my teeth, feeling super hot, super bored, and really resentful because Grandmama and her friends never told the sorry-ass preachers to shut up and sit down somewhere.

My problem with church was I knew what could have been. Every other Wednesday, the older women of the church had something called Home Mission: they would meet at alternate houses, and bring their best food, their Bibles, notebooks, and their testimonies. There was no instrumental music at Home Mission, but those women, Grandmama's friends, used their lives, their mo(u)rning songs, and their Bibles as primary texts to boast, confess, and critique their way into tearful silence every single time.

I didn't understand hell, partially because I didn't believe any place could be hotter than Mississippi in August. But I understood feeling good. I did not feel good at Concord Missionary Baptist church. I felt good watching Grandmama and her friends love each other during Home Mission.

When we pulled into our yard, Grandmama told me to grab the basket of nasty clothes and put it next to the washer. I picked the clothes up and instead of stopping at the washer, I walked into the kitchen, placed the dirty clothes basket on the floor in between the fridge and the oven.

I looked around to see if Grandmama was coming before stepping both of my penny loafers deep into the Mumfords' basket and doing "quick feet" like we did at the beginning of basketball and football practice. "I got your gun right here, white nigga," I said, stomping my feet all up in the white folks' clothes as hard and fast as I could. "Y'all don't even know. I got your gun right here, white nigga."

I was doing quick feet in the Mumfords' clothes for a good thirty seconds when Grandmama came out of nowhere, whupping my legs with a pleather blue belt. The little pleather blue licks didn't stop me. I was still doing quick feet like it was going out of style.

"Kie," Grandmama said, "get out my kitchen acting like a starnated fool."

I stopped and took my whupping. Afterward, I asked Grandmama whether she meant "star-nated" or "stark naked." I told her I'd rather be a "star-nated" fool because I loved stars even though I didn't think "star-nated" was a word. Grandmama and I loved talking about words. She was better than anyone I'd ever known at bending, breaking, and building words that weren't in the dictionary. I asked her what word I could use to make that Mumford boy feel what we felt.

"Ain't no need to make up words for words that already exist, Kie," she said. "That ain't nothing but the white you saw in that po' child today. And you don't want to feel no kinds of white. I feel sorry for them folk."

I looked at Grandmama and told her I felt like a nigger, and feeling like a nigger made my heart, lungs, kidneys, and brain feel like they were melting and dripping out the ends of my toenails.

"It ain't about making white folk feel what you feel," she said. "It's about not feeling what they want you to feel. Do you hear me? You better know from whence you came and forget about those folk." Grandmama started laughing. "Kie, what you call yourself doing to those folks' clothes?"

"Oh," I said, and start doing it again. "At practice, we be calling this quick feet."

"You gave them white-folk clothes them quick feets?"

"Not feets," I said, laughing. "It's already plural, Grandmama. Quick feet."

"Quick feets?" she said again, and kept laughing until she almost fell out of her chair. "Quick foots?"

"Grandmama," I told her, and sat next to her legs. "I hate white-folk clothes. I'm serious."

"I know you do." Grandmama stopped laughing. "I don't much appreciate them or they clothes either, but cleaning them nasty clothes is how we eat, and how I got your mama and them through school. You know I been washing them folks' clothes for years and I ain't never seen one washcloth?"

"What you mean, Grandmama?"

"I mean what I said. Them folk don't use no washcloths." I waited for a blink, a smirk, a slow roll of her eyes. I got nothing. "And the one time the little po' one who was messing with you asked me how to use a washrag, I told that baby, 'if you bring that washrag from your ass to your face, that's between you and your God.' And this baby just stood there laughing like I'm telling jokes. You know I was serious as a heart attack, Kie."

While I was dying laughing, Grandmama told me she whupped me for acting up in her kitchen, not for messing up them folks' clothes. She said she spent so many hours in white-folk kitchens and just wanted her children to respect her kitchen when she got home.

I asked Grandmama why she whupped me on my legs when I was doing quick feet, and not my head or my neck or my back like you would. "Because I don't want to hurt you," she said. "I want you to act like you got good sense but I don't ever want to hurt you."

Grandmama stood up and told me to follow her out to her garden. We went outside and picked butter beans, purple hull peas, collard greens, green tomatoes, and yellow squash.

"You know why I love my garden, Kie?"

"Because you don't want to have to rely on white folk to eat?"

"Chile, please," Grandmama said, walking back to the porch. "I ain't studdin' nan one of those folk when I'm at my own house. I love knowing directly what the food that be going in us has been through. You know what I mean?"

"I think I do," I told Grandmama as we sat on the porch, hulling peas and talking more about quick feet. My bucket of peas was between my legs when Grandmama stood up and straddled my tub.

"Kie, try hulling like this here," Grandmama said. I looked up at her hands and how they handled the purple hull peas. When she reached for my face, I jumped back. "I ain't trying to hurt you," she said. "What you jumping back for?"

I didn't know what to say.

Grandmama took the bucket from between my legs into the kitchen. I sat there looking at my hands. They wouldn't stop shaking. I felt sweat pooling up between my thighs. My body remembered what happened yesterday, and strangely knew what would happen tomorrow.

At supper, Grandmama apologized again for whupping my legs and told me when I wrote my report on the Book of Psalms later that night, I could write the way we talk. Like you, Grandmama made me do written assignments every night. Unlike your assignments, all of Grandmama's assignments had to be about the Bible.

Later that evening, I wrote, "I know you want me to write about the Book of Psalms. If it is okay I just want to tell you about some secrets that be making my head hurt. I be eating too much and staying awake at night and fighting people in Jackson. Mama does not like how my eyes are red. I wake her up in the morning and she be making me use Visine before school. I try but I can't tell her what's wrong. Can I tell you? Can you help me with my words? The words Mama make me use don't work like they supposed to work."

I wrote the words "be kissing me in the morning" "be choking me" "be running a train" "be beating my back" "be hearing her heartbeat" "be slow dancing with me" "be rubbing her breasts in my mouth" "be abandoning her" "be wet dreaming about stuff that scare me" "be watching people" "be getting beaten" "be listening to trains" "be on top of me" "be on my knees" "be kissing me in the morning" "be choking me" "be kissing him at night" "be hitting hard" "be saying white folk hit the hardest" "be laughing so it won't hurt" "be eating when I'm full" "be kissing me" "be choking me" "be confusing me."

At the end, I wrote, "Grandmama, can you please help me with my words?" I gave Grandmama my notebook when I was done like I had to every Sunday night we spent together. Unlike on other nights, she didn't say anything about what I'd written. When she walked by me, I didn't even hear her breathing.

Later that night, before bed, Grandmama got on her knees, turned the light off, and told me she loved me. She told me tomorrow would be a better day. Grandmama looked at that old raggedy gold and silver contraption she called her phone book before she got in bed with me like she always did. She looked up your name and number, Aunt Sue's name and number, Uncle Jimmy's name and number, and Aunt Linda's name and number.

Before both of us went to sleep, I asked Grandmama if 218 pounds was too fat for twelve years old. "What you weighing yourself for anyway?" she asked me. "Two hundred eighteen pounds is just right, Kie. It's just heavy enough."

"Heavy enough for what?"

"Heavy enough for everything you need to be heavy enough for."

I loved sleeping with Grandmama because that was the only place in the world I slept all the way through the night. But tonight was different. "Can I ask you one more question before we go to bed?"

"Yes, baby," Grandmama said, and faced me for the first time since I gave her the notebook. "What do you think about counting to ten in case of emergencies?"

"Ain't no emergency God can't help you forget," Grandmama told me. "Evil is real, Kie."

"But what about the emergencies made by folk who say they love you?"

"You forget it all," she said. "Especially that kind of emergency. Or you go stone crazy. My whole life, it seem like something crazy always happens on Sunday nights in the summer."

Grandmama made me pray again that night. I prayed for you to never close the door to your room if Malachi Hunter was there. I prayed for Layla and Dougie to never feel like they had to go back in Daryl's room. I prayed for Grandmama to have more money so she wouldn't have to stand in that big room ripping the bloody guts out of chickens before standing in that smaller room smelling bleach and white folks' shitty underwear. I prayed nothing would ever happen again in any room in the world that made us feel like we were dying.

When I got off my knees, I watched the back of Grandmama's body heave in and heave out as she fell asleep on the bed. Grandmama was trying, hard as she could, to forget one more Sunday night in the summer. For a second, though, she stopped heaving. I couldn't hear her breathing. When I finally climbed into bed, I placed my left thumb lightly on the small of Grandmama's back. She jerked forward and clenched the covers tighter around her body.

"My bad, Grandmama. I just wanted to make sure you were okay."

"Be still, Kie," Grandmama mumbled with her back to me. "Just be still. Close your eyes. Some things, they ain't meant to be remembered. Be still with the good things we got, like all them quick foots."

"Quick feet," I told her. "It's already plural. I know you know that, Grandmama. Quick feet."

II.

BLACK ABUNDANCE.

MEAGER

You were on your way back from Hawaii with Malachi Hunter while LaThon Simmons and I sat in the middle of a white eighth-grade classroom, in a white Catholic school, filled with white folk we didn't even know. These white folk watched us toss black vocabulary words, a dull butter knife, and pink grapefruit slices back and forth until it was time for us to go home.

We were new eighth graders at St. Richard Catholic School in Jackson, Mississippi, because Holy Family, the poor all-black Catholic school we attended most of our lives, closed unexpectedly due to lack of funding. All four of the black girls from Holy Family were placed in one homeroom at St. Richard. All three of us black boys from Holy Family were placed in another. Unlike at Holy Family, where we could wear what we wanted, at St. Richard, students had to wear khaki or blue pants or skirts and light blue, white, or pink shirts.

LaThon, who we both thought looked just like a slew-footed K-Ci from Jodeci, and I sat in the back of homeroom the first day of school doing what we always did: we intentionally used and misused last year's vocabulary words while LaThon cut up his pink grapefruit with his greasy, dull butter knife. "These white folk know we here on discount," he told me, "but they don't even know."

"You right," I told him. "These white folk don't even know

that you an ol' grapefruit-by-the-pound-eating-ass nigga. Give me some grapefruit. Don't be *parsimonious* with it, either."

"Nigga, you don't eat grapefruits," LaThon said. "Matter of fact, tell me one thing you eat that don't got butter in it. Ol' churning-your-own-butter-ass nigga." I was dying laughing. "Plus, you act like I got grapefruits gal-low up in here. I got one grapefruit."

Seth Donald, a white boy with two first names, looked like a dustier Shaggy from Scooby-Doo, but with braces. Seth spent the first few minutes of the first day of school silent-farting and turning his eyelids inside out. He asked both of us what "gal-low" meant.

"It's like *galore*," I told him, and looked at LaThon. "Like grapefruits *galore*."

LaThon sucked his teeth and rolled his eyes. "Seth, whatever your last name is, first of all, your first name ends with two *f*'s from now on, and your new name is Seff six-two because you five-four but you got the head of a nigga we know who six-two." LaThon tapped me on the forearm. "Don't he got a head like S. Slawter?" I nodded up and down as LaThon shifted and looked right in Seff 6'2's eyes. "Everythang about y'all is *erroneous*. Every. Thang. This that black *abundance*. Y'all don't even know."

LaThon's favorite vocab word in seventh grade was "abundance," but I'd never heard him throw "black" and "that" in front of it until we got to St. Richard.

While LaThon was cutting his half into smaller slices, he looked at me and said Seth six-two and them didn't even know about the slicing "shhhtyle" he used.

Right as I dapped LaThon up, Ms. Reeves, our white homeroom teacher, pointed at LaThon and me. Ms. Reeves looked like a much older version of Wendy from the Wendy's restaurants. We looked at each other, shook our heads, and kept cutting our grapefruit slices. "Put the knife away, LaThon," she said. "Put it down. Now!"

"Mee-guh," we said to each other. "Meager," the opposite of LaThon's favorite word, was my favorite word at the end of seventh grade. We used different pronunciations of meager to describe people, places, things, and shhhtyles that were at least eight levels less than nothing. "Mee-guh," I told her again, and pulled out my raggedy Trapper Keeper. "Mee-guh."

While Ms. Reeves was still talking, I wrote "#1 tape of our #1 group?" on a note and passed it to LaThon. He leaned over and wrote, "EPMD and *Strictly Business*." I wrote, "#1 girl you wanna marry?" He wrote, "Spinderalla + Tootie." I wrote, "#1 white person who don't even know?" LaThon looked down at his new red and gray Air Maxes, then up at the ceiling. Finally, he shook his head and wrote, "Ms. Reeves + Ronald Reagan. It's a tie. With they meager ass."

I balled up the note and put it in my too-tight khakis while Ms. Reeves kept talking to us the way you told me white folk would talk to us if we weren't perfect, the way I saw white women at the mall and police talk to you whether you'd broken the law or not.

I understood how Ms. Reeves had every reason in her world to think I was a sweaty, red-eyed underachiever who drank half a Mason jar of box wine before coming to school. That's almost exactly who I was. But LaThon was as close to abundant as an eighth grader could be.

LaThon brilliantly said "skrrimps" instead of "shrimp" because "skrrimps" just sounded better. He added three *s*'s to "mine" so it sounded like "minessss" no matter where we were. I once watched him tear open a black-and-white TV and make it into a bootleg version of Frogger and a miniature box fan for his girlfriend. One Friday in seventh grade, I saw him make the freshest paper airplane in the history of paper airplanes in Jackson. For five minutes and forty-six seconds, that plane soared, flipped, and dipped while LaThon and I ran underneath it for three blocks down Beaverbrook Drive. When the plane finally landed, LaThon kept looking up at the sky, wondering how the pocket of wind that carried our plane could find its way into a city like Jackson. LaThon could do anything, but the thing I'd never seen him do was come close to hurting someone who hadn't hurt him first, with a knife, his hands, or even his words.

"It's not a knife. It's a butter knife," I told Ms. Reeves. "And it's dull. Why she acting like a nigga got fine *cutlery* up in here?"

"You know," LaThon said. " 'Cause they *preposterous* in this school."

"*Preposterous*-er than a mug," I told Ms. Reeves, looking directly at Jabari, the other Holy Family black boy in our homeroom. LaThon and I knew it was against the West Jackson law for Jabari to get in trouble in school, so we didn't take it personally when he didn't stand up for us. LaThon got whuppings from his grandmama. I got beatings from you. Jabari could get beat the fuck up by his father when he got home. In Jackson, getting a whupping was so much gentler than getting a beating, and getting a beating was actually ticklish compared to getting beat the fuck up.

Ms. Reeves marched out of the room to get Ms. Stockard, a white teacher who'd subbed a few times at Holy Family. Ms. Stockard watched LaThon, Jabari, and me eat grapefruits with actual silver knives plenty of times at Holy Family and never said a word.

But it didn't matter.

"This isn't how we wanted you guys to start the year," she said as we all walked to the principal's office to call you and call LaThon's grandparents.

I sat in the principal's office thinking about what you told me the day before we started St. Richard. "Be twice as excellent and be twice as careful from this point on," you said. "Everything you thought you knew changes tomorrow. Being twice as excellent as white folk will get you half of what they get. Being anything less will get you hell."

I assumed we were already twice as excellent as the white kids at St. Richard precisely because their library looked like a cathedral and ours was an old trailer on cinder blocks. I thought you should have told me to be twice as excellent as you or Grandmama since y'all were the most excellent people I knew.

LaThon got whupped by a black woman who loved him when he got home. I got beaten by a black woman who loved me the next morning. With every lash you brought down on my body, I was reminded of what I knew, and how I knew it. I knew you didn't want white folk to judge you if I came to school with visible welts, so you beat me on my back, my ass, my thick thighs instead of my arms, my neck, my hands, and my face like you did when I went to Holy Family. I knew that if my white classmates were getting beaten at home, they were not getting beaten at home because of what any black person on Earth thought of them.

The next day at school, the teachers at St. Richard made sure LaThon and I never shared a classroom again. At St. Richard, the only time we saw each other was during recess, at lunch, or after school. When LaThon and I saw each other, we dapped each other up, held each other close as long as we could.

"It's still that black abundance?" I asked LaThon.

"You already know," he said, annunciating every syllable in a voice he'd never used before walking into his homeroom.

After school, in the front seat of our Nova, you told me what white folk demanded of us was never fair, but following their rules was sometimes safer for all the black folk involved and all the black folk coming after us. You kept talking about how amazing it was that Mississippi had just elected its first progressive governor since William Winter. You worked on Governor Mabus's campaign and kept talking about how much was possible politically in Mississippi because it was the blackest state in the nation.

"A third of white voters in Mississippi came out and did the right thing," you said. "That's all you need when thirty-three percent of your electorate is black and we get our folks out to the polls. Do you understand what's possible if we actually get effective radical politicians in place down here?"

"I understand it now because you've told me the same thing every day for the last year. I'm glad Mabus won, but hearing about it every day is just kinda mee-guh."

"Me what?" you asked me, cocking your hand back. "What did you say to me, Kie?"

"Me nothing," I said. "Me nothing."

Somewhere around our third quarter, Ms. Stockard made us read William Faulkner and Eudora Welty stories and watch *Roots* for black history month. I was the only Holy Family kid in my English class. Ms. Stockard talked a lot about the work of Eudora Welty all year. She talked a lot about "historical context" when speaking about the "quirky racism" of Welty's characters and compared quirky racism to the "bad real racism" of most of the white characters in *Roots*. I didn't like what "historical context" and "quirky racism" in our English class granted white folk. If we could understand historical context, we could understand how Eudora Welty could create fully developed, unreliable white protagonists who treated partially developed black objects like "niggers." I felt the weight of "historical context," "quirky racism," and "bad real racism" in that eighth-grade classroom, but I also felt something else I was embarrassed to admit. I felt a tug toward the interior of Welty's stories.

Even though there were bold boundaries between my imagination and Welty's, when she started "Why I Live at the P.O." with the sentence "I was getting along fine with Mama, Papa-Daddy and Uncle Rondo until my sister Stella-Rondo just separated from her husband and came back home again," I didn't just feel an intimate relationship to Welty's text; I felt every bit of Jackson, and really every bit of Mississippi you taught me to fear.

Welty didn't know a lick about Mississippi black folk, but she knew enough about herself to mock white folk in the most ruthlessly petty ways I'd ever read. You and Grandmama taught me white folk were capable of anything and not to be provoked, but Welty reminded me of what my eyes and ears taught me: white folk were scared and scary as all hell, so scared, so scary the words "scared" and "scary" weren't scared or scary enough to describe them.

I didn't hate white folk. I didn't fear white folk. I wasn't easily impressed or even annoyed by white folk because even before I met actual white folk, I met every protagonist, antagonist, and writer of all the stories I ever read in first, second, third, fourth, fifth, sixth, seventh, and eighth grade. At the same time, I met Wonder Woman, the narrator on *The Wonder Years*, Ricky from *Silver Spoons*, Booger from *Revenge of the Nerds*, Spock from *Star Trek*, Mallory from *Family Ties*, damn near all the coaches and owners of my favorite teams. I met Captain America, Miss America, "The American Dream" Dusty Rhodes. I met Luke Skywalker and his white father, even though his white father's voice, outfit, and mask were blacker than thirty-seven midnights. I met poor white folk, rich white folk, and middle-class white folk. I met all the Jetsons, all the Flintstones, all the Beverly Hillbillies, the entire Full House, damn near everyone in Pee Wee's Playhouse, all American presidents, the dudes they said were Jesus and Adam, the women they said were the Virgin Mary and Eve, and all the characters on Grandmama's stories except for Angie and Jessie from *All My Children*. So even if we didn't know real white folk, we knew a lot of the characters white folk wanted to be, and we knew who we were to those characters.

That meant we knew white folk.

That meant white folk did not know us.

The next day in English class, we watched the scene where Kizzy, Kunta Kinte's daughter on *Roots*, was raped by this white man named Tom Moore. The morning after the rape, a black woman played by Helen from *The Jeffersons* came by to wash Kizzy's wounds.

Helen told Kizzy, "You best know about Master Tom Mo'. He's one of them white mens that likes nigger women . . . Reckon he be bothering you most every night now. Used to bother me, but no mo'."

I wasn't sure what to do with what I just heard. The first time I watched that *Roots* scene, I was eight years old. I remember hearing "rake" instead of "rape" when I asked you what happened to Kizzy. "Raking" someone sounded like the scariest thing that could happen to a person. I didn't understand why Helen sounded sad that Tom Mo' wouldn't be raking her anymore. I asked you why anyone would "rake" another person. "Because some men do not care if they hurt other people's bodies," you said. "Some men want to feel what they want to feel when they want to feel it because it hurts other people, not in spite of it hurting people."

Tom Mo' was white. But he was a man. I was black. But I was a boy who other black men called li'l man. I didn't think I would ever do to Kizzy what Tom Mo' did. But I wondered if I would feel pressure to do that when I grew up. And if I could do what Tom Mo' did, were Tom Mo' and me different to Kizzy? I wondered what Layla would have felt if three white random dudes walked her into Daryl's bedroom that day, and not three black dudes we knew. I didn't know how to think about it and not knowing how to think about it made my head hurt, and made me want to eat boxes of off-brand strawberry Pop-Tarts.

At recess that day, the St. Richard white boys moved with the same eager stiffness they always moved with during break. A lot of the white girls at St. Richard and all of us Holy Family kids moved like we'd had a burning secret poured into our ears.

LaThon and I found Shalaya Odom, Madra, Baraka, and Hasanati sitting in a circle, quietly looking at each other's feet. I'd never seen them sit silently at Holy Family. Shalaya Odom didn't usually cuss much at all, but when I asked her what was wrong, she said, "That *Roots* shit, I had my ears covered the whole time."

73

LaThon said we should go find Jabari and make sure he was okay. Jabari was the best writer at Holy Family. Out of all of us Holy Family kids, Jabari made the easiest transition to St. Richard. He really wanted to sleep in white-folk houses, ride in white-folk cars, and eat white-folk food.

We walked in the building and thought maybe Jabari was talking to Ms. Stockard about writing fiction, since that was something he liked to do during recess. When we walked in her room, Ms. Stockard said she was glad we came to talk to her because she'd been wanting to talk to us for a few weeks.

"Guys, I really want to be respectful," she said, sipping on a warm Tab cola. "How is Jabari doing?" We both looked at each other without blinking. "Listen, I need you guys to tell Jabari to take a shower or a bath before coming to school. Maybe a bath at night and a shower or wash-up in the morning. Some students and a few teachers came to talk to me about, you know, his odor. It's really grossing every-one out."

We laughed out loud at first because there was nothing funnier than hearing your white teacher talk about how stanky one of your boys was.

"Ms. Stockard, are you trying to say Jabari stank?" I asked her. "Because we heard a rumor that white folk don't use washcloths no way."

LaThon burst out laughing.

"I'm not saying anything about"—she used her hands to make air quotes—"'stank' or washcloths. I'm saying some people think Jabari is just gross. You guys can understand how that is not good for any of you, right?"

LaThon and I stood silently next to each other. I wasn't sure how a teacher could teach a kid they thought was gross.

I didn't know why Jabari's stank was okay at Holy Family but somehow gross at St. Richard. I knew Jabari smelled at St. Richard the same way Jabari smelled at Holy Family, the same way he smelled ever since his mother died. It wasn't his odor, and it wasn't that he didn't take showers or use washcloths. Ever since his mother died, there was just a different scent as soon as you walked in Jabari's house. And if you stayed longer than thirty minutes, you left smelling like Jabari's house. But all of us were stanky at some point, even Shalaya Odom. When we were stanky, we laughed about it, took a shower, or threw some deodorant, cologne, or perfume on top of the stank and kept it moving.

I understood, swaying there in front of Ms. Stockard, that all of us at Holy Family shared stories with words, word patterns, vocal inflections, and really, bodies that made us feel safe. No one at Holy Family ever used their bodies to say "awesome" or "totally" or "amazing" or "FUBAR" or "like" fifty times a day more than necessary. The narrators of our stories said "fly" and "all that" and "fresh" and "the shit" and "sheiiiit" and "shole" and "shining" and "trippin'" and "all-world" and "living foul" and "musty" and "sorry-ass" and "stale" and "ashy" and "getting full" and "cuhrazee" and "nigga" and "you know what I'm saying" fifty times a day more than necessary.

There wasn't a "gross" or anything approximating a "gross" in our vocabulary, or our stories. Bodies at Holy Family were heavier than the bodies at St. Richard. And none of those heavy bodies were gross. Seventh grade was the first year in our lives when boys started calling girls who wouldn't give us any attention words like "freak" behind their backs. And when they slapped the taste out our mouth, we apologized. But even in our most brittle whispers, we never thought or talked about any girl's body as "gross." Or maybe I wanted that to be true. At the end of seventh grade, the same day we went to sing Club Nouveau songs at the old-folk home, Shalaya Odom stood up and walked out with a dark brown stain on the back of her jean skirt. We thought she'd shit on herself until LaThon explained she might have just started her period. We never called Shalaya Odom gross but we laughed in a way the girls at Holy Family would not have laughed at us if we actually had unexpected chunky shit dripping down our legs.

Worse than any cuss word we could imagine, "gross" existed on the other side of what we considered abundant. And in the world we lived in and loved, everyone black was in some way abundant. We'd all listened to grown-folk spade sessions on Fridays. We'd all dressed in damn near our Easter best to watch the pregame, the game, and, mostly, the halftime show of Jackson State vs. Valley, Valley vs. Alcorn, Alcorn vs. Southern, or Grambling vs. Jackson State on Saturday. Saturday night, we'd all driven back home in the backseats of cars, listening to folk theorize about the game, Mississippi politics, and why somebody's auntie and uncle were trying to sell their child's World's Finest Chocolates in the parking lot after the game. Sunday morning, we'd all been dragged into some black church by our parents and grandparents. And every Sunday, we hoped to watch some older black folk fan that black heathen in tennis shoes who caught the Holy Spirit. But outside of stadiums and churches, and outside of weekends, we were most abundant. While that abundance dictated the shape and movement of bodies, the taste and texture of our food, it was most apparent in the way we dissembled and assembled words, word sounds, and sentences.

LaThon and I loved Jabari too much to tell him Ms. Stockard and some other white kids whose smiles, words, and food he loved thought he was gross. Instead of saying any of what I was really feeling to Ms. Stockard, a white woman who had the power to get us beaten by black women who loved us and distrusted her, I said, "We understand, Ms. Stockard. We will tell Jabari to take more wash-ups before he comes to school."

Later that day, near the end of practice, my basketball coach, Coach Gee, the father of Donnie Gee, one of the only black boys at St. Richard, brought out a scale so we could weigh ourselves. We were going to a tournament in Vicksburg and the organizers needed our weight and height for the program.

I hadn't weighed myself since stepping on the scale at the Mumfords' earlier in the summer. I hated public scales, but I made myself believe I was under 210 pounds for the first time in three years.

I stepped on the scale.

170.

175.

180.

185.

190.

Shit.

200.

210.

215.

225.

228.

"Damn," Coach Gee said, looking at the rest of the team. "This big joker weigh two hundred thirty-one pounds!"

I walked away from the scale, faked a smile, and watched the rest of the team laugh. I went to the bathroom, made myself pee twice, and walked back to the scale.

"Two hundred thirty-one," Coach Gee said again. "It ain't the scale, Baby Barkley. Shit. It's you."

After practice, I tried to hold my stomach in and put dry clothes over my wet musty practice uniform. For the first time in my life, I thought about the sweat and fat between my thighs, the new stretch marks streaking toward my nipples. I felt fat before. I felt husky every day of my life. I'd never felt what I felt in that St. Richard bathroom.

"Damn, nigga," LaThon said as I walked out of the gym. His grandfather was picking us up and taking us home. "Everybody trippin' because you weigh like twenty-six more pounds than Michael Jordan, but you like eight inches shorter?"

I didn't say anything.

"Wait, I know my nigga ain't acting all sensitive over no scale. You ain't gross. You know that, right? You ain't gross. You just a heavy nigga who quicker than most skinny niggas we know. You ain't gross. You hear me? You you."

Later that weekend, LaThon and I met Jabari in his backyard over in Presidential Hills. LaThon hyped this soft-ass dunk Jabari did on his younger brother, Stacey. He called the dunk "the Abundance" and I gave Jabari the nickname "Kang Slender." Jabari tucked his bottom lip under his front teeth and flew through the air doing awkward versions of "the Abundance" until the sun went down. Every time he dunked, LaThon and I laughed and laughed and laughed until we didn't. Eventually, Jabari laughed with us when LaThon said, "They don't even know about the Abundance. For real. We can't even be mad. They don't even know."

"We can be mad," Jabari said. "But we can be other stuff, too."

We both looked at Jabari and waited for him to say more. I was finally understanding, for all that bouncy talk of ignorance and how they didn't really know, that white folk, especially grown white folk, knew exactly what they were doing. And if they didn't, they should have.

But by the end of February of our eighth-grade year, what white folk at St. Richard and the world knew didn't matter. We were learning how to suck our teeth, shake our heads, frame a face for all occasions like Richard III, and laugh each other whole. That meant a lot. Mostly, it meant that although some of us had more welts on our bodies than lunch money, light bill money, or money for our discounted tuition, we knew we were not the gross ones.

We were mad, and sometimes sad, but we were other stuff, too.

On the way out of Jabari's house that day, I grabbed a T-shirt from his dirty clothes. I was well into an XL, while Jabari's and LaThon's bird chests barely filled out a smedium. But I was learning from you how to make anything, regardless the size or shape, bend. I came to school the rest of that year with my breasts, my love handles, and my stomach compressed in a T-shirt that smelled so much like Jabari's house. When white folk at St. Richard looked at me like I was gross, I smiled, shook my head, sucked my teeth, intentionally misused and mispronounced some vocabulary words. Then I dapped LaThon up at lunch and said, "They so meager and we so gross. I'm talking about we *so* gross. It's still that black abundance?"

"Yup," LaThon told me. "And they still don't even know."

CONTRACTION

While I was shaking my head, sucking my teeth, and mumbling Ice Cube lyrics on the bench of the junior varsity basketball team at DeMatha Catholic High in Hyattsville, Maryland, you were realizing your academic dream of earning a postdoc fellowship in College Park, Maryland.

On the way home from a basketball game where you went off on Coach Ricks for benching me in the fourth quarter, we stopped to eat at Western Sizzler. I was supposed to be eating salads. "That white boy, your coach," you said, "what is his name, Kie? Micks?"

"Ricks."

"Coach Ricks is so intimidated. I'll take a dumb white boy over a smug, insecure white boy any day of the year."

"Intimidated by what?"

"What aren't they intimidated by? I'm a black woman with a PhD and a postdissertation fellowship from a major university." I told you I didn't think anyone other than you and four other people even knew what that meant. "At some point, you are going to have to understand that people outside of Mississippi never know what to do with us when we're excellent. So they do what they can to punish us."

I sat in the booth of the restaurant, musty, screw-faced, trying to make sense of what you said. None of it really made sense but I was happy to learn we were this contentious thick-thighed Mississippi duo facing a slew of northern enemies trying to punish us for shining.

"They cannot fuck with us," you kept saying. "Excuse me for saying it. But it's true. They cannot fuck with us."

On the way back to our apartment that night, I thought about how the black boys at DeMatha call me a "Bama," how the coaches and students made fun of how I pronounced the word "am-bue-lance," how my Spanish teacher joked with the rest of the class that my blazer smelled like catfish, and how all my teachers, who all happen to be white men, patted me on the head in class and said "Good for you, Kee-say" when I got an obvious answer right.

When we were half a mile from home, a Maryland police car stopped us. Just like when they stopped us in Mississippi, you sat up in your seat, kept both hands on the wheel, and looked straight ahead. You took out your University of Maryland ID and tucked my red, black, and green African medallion into my Public Enemy T-shirt. You told me to sit up, keep my hands on the dashboard, and don't say a word.

The officer knelt down and looked in your window. When I saw your face so close to his gun, I wanted to snatch it and watch it melt into black grits. Ever since police started approaching me more often in Mississippi, I wanted the superpower to melt every gun in the world into black grits. The officer asked why we had Mississippi license plates.

"Because we are residents of Jackson, Mississippi," you said. "I have a postdoctoral appointment at the University of Maryland at College Park. Have I done anything wrong, Officer?"

When the officer told you to speak up and claimed you changed lanes without signaling, you kept your grip on the

steering wheel and said, "I did not change lanes without signaling. You sped up behind me so I signaled and changed
lanes."

The officer tried to laugh in your face as he asked for
license and registration. "Is that your man?" he asked you.
"He needs to show identification, too."

Your hands came off the steering wheel and you pointed at
the officer's face. "Move away from my car," you said. "That
is my child and he is fifteen years old. He does not have identification. May I have your badge number, please?" I hated how
it sounded when you didn't use contractions.

The officer asked both of us to step out of the car.

"We will not get out of this car," you said, louder this time.
"We have done nothing wrong."

My fists were balled up, and I was inching toward the
driver-side window. You slapped me across my chest with the
back of your hand, and told me to be quiet and unclench my
fists right as another officer pulled up. The first officer, who
was now laughing, walked back to the second officer's car.

You eventually showed the second officer your license and
your University of Maryland ID. The officer looked at the ID,
flipped it over, and told us to have a good night.

"Never give them a chance to take the shot," you finally
said after we walked in the apartment and locked the door.
"They will take it. They will take it. They will take it." I wondered why you said it three times, and why you never told me
to shoot back. "Mississippi. Maryland. It don't matter where
you are. They will shoot your black ass out of the sky every
chance they get. If you have a heart attack dodging their bul-
lets, they will hide they guns and say you killed yourself."

"I hear you," I told you, and tried to make you laugh.

"Why didn't you just say 'don't' instead of 'does not' or 'doesn't' and 'they' instead of 'their,' though?"

"If I did not know correct English, it's more likely that police officer might have shot us," you said.

"No he wouldn't," I told you. "That fool got madder *because* you were speaking correct English."

You looked at me like you were thinking. "You might actually be right, Kie. But in the long run, correct English will save a black man more than it will hurt you."

"Will correct English save you, though?"

"I do not need saving," you said. "I am not the one who is an endangered species."

"I'm not either," I told you. "I'm an endangered species with a lot of gas in my stomach. I'll be right back. That cop gave me the bubble-guts."

You laughed and laughed and laughed until you didn't.

While I was in my room changing, you told me to write about what I learned from the experience with the police. I wasn't sure what to write because I wasn't sure how to live life in a way that didn't give them a chance to shoot us out of the sky. It seemed like just driving, or walking into a house, or doing your job, or cutting a grapefruit was all it took to get shot out of the sky. And the biggest problem was police weren't the only people doing the shooting. They were just the only people allowed to walk around and threaten us with guns and prison if they didn't like our style of flying.

I loved our style of flying.

During the Christmas break, LaThon took me to Murrah High School, where we watched a six-nine tenth grader we knew named Othella make every shot he attempted in warm-ups, the first half, and halftime of the game. Othella finished with over forty points, twelve dunks, and over twenty rebounds. He hardly played the fourth quarter. LaThon and I watched the game completely silent.

"You know they say Othella the best tenth grader in the nation?" LaThon finally asked me on the way home.

"You mean best in Mississippi?"

"Naw, bruh. I mean the nation. The game done changed."

"Them busters at my school up in Maryland be calling us Bamas down here," I told him. "If we Bamas, how come we got the best tenth grader in the nation? Plus we got Hollywood Robinson and Chris Jackson."

"Walter Payton," LaThon said.

"Fannie Lou Hamer."

"Even if we look at white boys, we got Brett Favre."

"And Oprah," I told him. "Oprah 'bout to be bigger than Barbara Walters out here. They trippin'."

"Yeah," LaThon said, "they stay trippin' but what we gone do? Me and you."

That night, LaThon and I realized the basketball we'd been playing and the basketball Othella played weren't the same basketball. We loved playing ball, but Othella was a baller. Thanks to Othella Harrington, LaThon Simmons started imagining life as an engineer that night and I started imagining life as a middle school teacher whose side-hustl was rapping.

A few weeks after we returned to Maryland, I got caught cheating on a world history test Coach Ricks was proctoring. I cheated the day after I refused to read the world history book assigned and read a book called *Before the Mayflower* in class instead. You hadn't beaten me the whole time we'd been in Maryland but when you came to school to get me, I knew I'd get my back destroyed.

"I know what you're doing," you said when we got in the car. "Let it go."

"Let what go?" I asked you.

"Just let it go, Kie."

That was it. No lashes. No slaps. No lines.

You were happier than I'd ever seen you. You never came in my bedroom crying in the middle of the night. You gave me kisses on the face, cracked fart jokes, and held my hand when I least expected it.

"I'm not a teacher here," I heard you tell Grandmama a few times on the phone. "I'm just a scholar. I earned this time to write and research. That means a lot to me, Ma. I'm learning how to love Kie and myself the right way. Yeah, I guess it is better late than never."

I didn't understand what the "scholar" part of your sentence really meant. But in Maryland, for the first time since I'd known you, we didn't run out of gas. Our lights were never cut off. We didn't have a fridge full of food or much extra money, but we were never, ever hungry.

When I came back from playing ball at the Greenbelt rec center during spring break, you made me read back over sentences I'd written in my notebooks back in Mississippi. You said I asked a lot of questions about what I saw and heard in my writing, but because I didn't reread the questions I didn't push myself to different answers. You said a good question always trumps an average answer.

"The most important part of writing, and really life," you said, "is revision."

When you don't care about making other people feel pain, I'm wondering if you are being a violent person?

I wrote that sentence in Jackson and revised it the night Marion Barry was caught on TV smoking crack. I couldn't understand why you cried that night and kept saying, "This is all so violent. They're going to use this video to come after black elected officials for decades. Do your work, Kie. Revise, and never, ever let these people see you fail."

Nothing I'd read in school prepared me to think through the permanence of violence in Mississippi, Maryland, and the whole nation. After school, I kept reading and rearranging the words I'd written, trying to understand what the words meant for my understanding of violence. For the first time in my life, I realized telling the truth was way different from finding the truth, and finding the truth had everything to do with revisiting and rearranging words. Revisiting and rearranging words didn't only require vocabulary; it required will, and maybe courage. Revised word patterns were revised thought patterns. Revised thought patterns shaped memory. I knew, looking at all those words, that memories were there. I just had to rearrange, add, subtract, sit, and sift until I found a way to free the memory. You told me in Mississippi revision was practice. In Maryland, I finally believed you. The truth was that practicing writing meant practicing sitting down, sitting still, and my body did not ever want to be still. When it had to be still, all it wanted to do was imagine dunking with two hands or kissing a girl who loved me. Sitting still, just as much as any other part of writing, took practice. Most days, my body did not want to practice, but I convinced it that sitting still and writing were a path to memory.

I remembered writing down and memorizing tens of thousands of sentences written by rappers and wondering what it would feel like to write sentences black children wanted to memorize.

I remembered flying around Jackson, teeth chattering on command from LaThon's new subwoofer. I remember lounging in the passenger seat with "Criminal Minded" and "Dopeman" blasting, and LaThon leaning at a forty-five-degree angle in the driver's seat of his grandfather's Cutlass. I remembered LaThon saying, "You take that black shit too far sometimes," after I almost got a whole car of us shot for talking reckless to the police.

I remembered turning the volume up on our little black-and-white TV to watch *Benson* and *Night Court* when Malachi Hunter came to the house. I remember feeling petrified when Kamala Lackey asked me to touch her breasts in the art closet during second period in ninth grade. I remembered being okay never kissing a girl if I could touch myself to the thought of Layla, or Kamala Lackey asking me to touch her breasts in the art closet, for the rest of my life.

I remembered watching friends with hats cocked left shoot friends with hats cocked right. I remembered what it felt like to watch some of those friends disappear.

I remembered begging Grandmama to let me stay with her when you told me we had to leave Mississippi for a year. I remembered sitting on Grandmama's porch and watching her tell me she was going to be lonely while we're gone. I remembered forgiving you when Grandmama told me you beat me so much because something in Jackson was beating you.

I remembered waking up one morning wondering where all the big boys in Beulah Beauford's house went. I remember finding out that two of them were in jail for selling drugs too close to a school, one of them was shipped out of the state, and that Layla had to move in with her grandparents in Memphis.

I remembered seeing Layla when she came back to Jackson for the homecoming game at Jackson State. I remembered asking her if she was mad at me for leaving her at Beulah Beauford's house that day. I remembered listening, and trying to look cool as Layla said, "All I wanted to do was swim, just like y'all. I ain't studdin' none of y'all niggas."

Before leaving Maryland, I went to a doctor for the second time in my life. The good news was the doctor said I was six-one, 208 pounds, two inches taller and almost twenty pounds lighter than I was when I left Jackson. The bad news was I had a murmur in my heart. You said even though the murmur was functional, I should be worried because we watched Hank Gathers, the power forward for the Loyola Marymount basketball team, die of a heart attack on television after catching an alley-oop.

I loved the sound of the word "murmur" and I loved that I was coming back to Mississippi with a murmur, a smaller body, and a new relationship to writing, revision, memory, and you.

America seems filled with violent people who like causing people pain but hate when those people tell them that pain hurts.

HULK

You were on one end of Grandmama's couch yelling at me while I was on the other end grasping the side of my face. We weren't back in Mississippi for longer than a week when you smashed me across my face with the heel of a Patrick Ewing Adidas because I talked back. The side of my face started to swell, but I couldn't understand why getting hit in the face with the heel of a Ewing didn't hurt as much as it had before we left Jackson. I was six-one, 215 pounds, nine inches taller and over forty pounds heavier than you. The softer parts of my heart and body were getting harder and those harder parts didn't want to hurt you, but they wanted to never, ever be hurt by you again.

I was heavier and taller than all of my friends' fathers, but the peach fuzz under my arms, thin patches of pubic hair, and no hair at all on my face didn't care how big my body was. Let the hair tell it, I was still a child while LaThon, Donnie Gee, Jabari, and them were all starting to grow full-fledged mustaches and beards. The weekend before school started, you promised me you'd take me to get a haircut Monday. When Monday came, I had to decide between lunch money for the week or a haircut. I chose lunch money for the week, and you convinced me you could give me the best at-home fade I'd ever seen. I'm not sure why I believed you. You had many gifts, but drawing straight lines with or without a ruler, staying in the lines while coloring in a coloring book were not some of those gifts.

I expected the fade would be a bit off, but you actually managed to give me the worst fade I'd ever seen on a human in Mississippi. It wasn't just that the fade didn't fade; it was that no part of the fade looked symmetrical. My eyes watered looking at my new haircut. I asked you to leave the bathroom while you laughed until you cried at my reaction to this fade that refused to fade. I locked the door and wondered what would happen if I shaved my head bald like Barkley and Jordan.

When I opened the door, you gasped and said a bald head would make white people and police think I was more of a threat.

"Good," I said, and closed the door again to wash all the hair off.

After I got out of the shower, I looked at my hairless head and face and wondered how I'd look, not with a huge Lamont Sanford mustache, but with just the shadow of a mustache like LaThon and them had. I opened the drawer, found your mascara, and smudged the coal across the skin above my top lip until my face joined my body in looking, and feeling, more like a man.

The entire ride to school, you kept talking about my bald head. I kept thinking about my new fake mustache. When I grabbed my bag and got ready to get out of the car, you said, "Be patient with your body, Kie. I love you." I remember wishing you'd been this version of yourself the day you clocked me across the face with a Patrick Ewing Adidas.

My first few months back in Jackson were spent moving my big bald-headed self from LaThon's couch, to Jabari's bottom bunk, to Donnie Gee's guest room, to varsity basketball practice at St. Joseph High School. One night, after a basketball game, a chubby white tenth grader with glassy eyes, a black convertible, and strong hands asked to buy me a banana shake. Her name was Abby Claremont. Two days later, in the back of Jabari's van, Abby asked me how many girls I'd kissed. After I lied and said about five—which was five more than the truth—Abby kissed me on my lips. A few weeks later, Abby asked me how many times I'd had sex. After I lied and said about four and a half—which was four and a half more than the truth—Abby asked me to have sex at Donnie Gee's house while his mother was at work.

Even though Abby didn't really know me, and I didn't really know her, I wanted to spend the rest of my life with her. I'd heard a lot about big boys cheating on their girlfriends but cheating confused me. I assumed all of those big boys knew sex with someone they loved felt the opposite of gross, the opposite of meager. It was actually the only thing in the world that felt nearly as good as that black abundance. I didn't understand how sex with someone you didn't love could feel nearly as good.

"Thank you," Abby said while we were lying in the bed after having sex the first time. "I know you were scared."

"How you know I was scared?" I asked her. "My rhythm was meager, huh? I can do better next time."

"Not at all," she said, and laughed until she started coughing. "I just know you were scared because I love you. I can tell you love me back. That's scary."

No other woman who touched me wanted to only be touched by me. All I wanted to do was make Abby feel as happy as she made me feel. I wondered what it meant to be touched and loved sexually by a white girl in Mississippi, but I was lost in what it felt to be touched and loved by any woman or girl in Mississippi other than you, Grandmama, and Renata. I always assumed the first woman I would have real sex with would be Layla, after I got older, got a decent job, and lost a lot of weight around my thighs.

LaThon called me a sellout and sucker when he found out about Abby Claremont. "We from Holy Family," he said. "We know better than to do that kind of shit. You forgot where we from?"

Instead of chilling with him after practice, or going to watch Mid-South Wrestling with him on Friday nights, I found ways to be with Abby Claremont. I wanted to talk to him about what my body felt during love and sex, and ask him if his body felt anything like mine. I wanted to know if he kept his shirt on when he had sex. How did he feel right before and right after orgasms? What did he do when sweat dripped in his eyes during sex? If his girlfriend wanted to have sex in the car, but he really needed to take a shower first, did he tell her he was musty so the stank wouldn't be a surprise? I wanted to tell LaThon I wasn't a sellout and I wasn't in love with a white girl but it was hard when I was doing sellout/in-love stuff like riding in her black convertible with the top down, or holding her hand in between classes, or watching her white friends use vowel sounds we prided ourselves on obliterating and never calling them meager to their faces.

The only other girl at my school who asked me to touch her was my friend Kamala Lackey. Kamala Lackey was husky, quick for her size, fine as all outdoors, darker than me, and the wittiest junior at St. Joseph. Like me, Kamala Lackey didn't have a car or a license. She lived twenty miles away in Canton.

So if Kamala Lackey was ever going to ask me to do anything other than hold her hand or touch her breasts in the art closet, we would have to do some serious planning. I was scared to plan or initiate anything with a girl because if a girl said yes to anything I planned, I wondered if it was because she was scared to say no because I was so heavy. I never wanted anyone to do anything with their body they didn't want to do. If Kamala Lackey kissed me first, I would have kissed her. If she asked me to have sex with her, I would have happily, and fearfully, done it. But I didn't know if I would have felt as free or defiant after Kamala Lackey and I had sex, though I know I would have felt as beautiful. Kamala Lackey reminded me every third period, "Abby Claremont got that big ol' jungle fever and you the big ol' jungle," since Abby's last boyfriend was a fat black boy like me. "I'm the big ol' jungle, too," she said. "Big ol' jungles need to be with big ol' jungles."

I laughed and laughed and laughed at Kamala Lackey's joke until I didn't.

I kept my relationship with Abby Claremont a secret because I knew you would beat me if you knew I was having sex with a white girl, but mostly because I didn't want you to think you'd raised a big black sellout who thought you were ugly. I wasn't completely sure I was a sellout, but I knew you were the most beautiful woman in the world. In my imaginary conversations with you, you shook your head and hugged me when I told you I just really liked having sex with a girl who only wanted to have sex with me, and Abby Claremont was the only person in the world for whom that was true. In my imagination, you kissed me on the cheek for saying "for whom."

Abby Claremont and I had sex a lot but we never asked

each other one question about our relationships to sex, other than "why don't you ever initiate" and "did that feel good to you?" I didn't know how to answer those questions and I worried if I said the wrong thing, Abby Claremont would think I was weak and wouldn't want to have sex with only me anymore.

Friday and Saturday nights, Abby and her friends hung out and got drunk in the parking lot of St. Richard. Sometimes I'd be the only black person there. On those days, I tried to stay in the car listening to the new Black Sheep tape until she was ready to leave or too drunk to know where she was. Abby Claremont wanted to have sex a lot of those nights when she was drunk. Usually, I said no because my body told me it was wrong. Once I said yes because I wanted to feel touched, but I didn't want to be judged if my touch was meager. The day after I had sex with Abby Claremont while she was drunk, I knew I'd done something wrong, though Abby Claremont told me she wanted to do everything we did. I just didn't know how she could remember anything we did.

When I told her I wanted to talk to her about having sex while she was drunk, she said, "I trust you. Don't worry about it. I know you'd never hurt me. I know you're a good dude."

Near the middle of the basketball season, I played like basketball wasn't the most important thing in my world. Our coach, Coach Phil Schitzler, a gravelly voiced white man who was also the most popular teacher in school, told Donnie Gee he thought my problem was "that white girl."

When I went to talk to Coach Schitzler, he demanded I get my priorities straight and stop running around after Abby Claremont. "It's in your best interest to not be running around chasing no nut with that fast-ass gal," he told me. "Wait till after the playoffs. Then you can chase all the nuts you want."

"Chasing a nut" became the phrase all my boys used to describe a person who was fiending for sex, but not fiending for a relationship. Even though LaThon knew I was a sellout, he died laughing every time I said, "That nigga stay chasing a nut." I never told him I stole "chasing a nut" from Coach Schitzler.

On March 4, 1991, a few weeks after we lost in the playoffs, I went to Jabari's house after open gym. Abby Claremont was going to pick me up later that night, have sex in the parking lot of Red Lobster, and take me to the end of my street, where I would walk home. While we were watching a basketball game, the news was interrupted with a video of a gang of white police officers surrounding four other white police officers. The four officers in the middle were beating the life out of this heavy-chained black man.

We watched the news replay the video four times.

We all had cops rough us up, chase us, pull guns on us, call us out of our names. We all watched cops shame our mamas, aunties, and grandmamas. We all floated down I-55 creating lyrical force fields from the police and everything the police protected and served, rapping, "A young nigga got it bad 'cause I'm brown." But here we were, in one of our safe spaces, watching white folk watch white police watch other white police destroy our body.

Abby Claremont's horn surprised me.

"What's wrong?" she asked as I got in her convertible.

"Nothing," I said, and kept picking around the minibag of Funyuns I took from Jabari's house. "Can we put the top up and can you just take me home?"

"Why?"

"My mama just said I have to be home earlier than usual. She sick. The flu."

"You are such a fucking liar, Keece," she said. "Tell me why you want the top up? I'm asking. And what is that smell?" I looked at her in a way I never looked at her before. "Why are you looking at me like that? Say it."

"Can we just talk about what we're doing tomorrow?"

Usually when I got out of Abby Claremont's convertible, we kissed on the lips with lots of tongue. Tonight, I kissed Abby Claremont on her cheek and told her thanks for being so nice to me. She started trying to talk to me about what was happening at home between her father and her mother, but I told her I could not talk about that right now because you were sick.

"Asshole," she said as I got out of the car. "Don't fucking call me tonight either. Or tomorrow."

When I got in the house, you brought your belt across my neck. Earlier in the day, Ms. Andrews, one of your friends who was a teacher at my school, told you Coach Schitzler said I was in a sexual relationship with a white girl. You heard this "news" on the same day you watched a gang of white police officers try to kill a chained black man they later claimed had "Hulk-like" strength.

I did not know Rodney King, but I could tell by how he wiggled, rolled, and ran he was not a Hulk. Hulks did not beg for mercy. Hulks did not shuffle from ass whuppings. Hulks had no memories, no mamas. I wondered what niggers and police were to a Hulk. I wondered if all sixteen-year-old Americans had a little Hulk in them.

I knew, or maybe I accepted, for the first time no matter

96

what anyone did to me, I would never beg anyone for mercy. I would always recover. There was physically nothing anyone could do to me to take my heart, other than kill me. You, Grandmama, and I had that same Hulk in our chest. We would always recover. At some point during my beating, I just stopped fighting and I let you hit me. I did not scream. I did not yell. I barely breathed. I took my shirt off without you telling me. I let you beat me across my back. It was the only beating in my life where watching you beat me as hard as you could felt good.

After the beating, you came to my bedroom. You told me I really needed to think about the difference between loving someone and loving how someone made me feel. You said if I liked how Abby Claremont made me feel, I really needed to ask myself why. You kept telling me I was beautiful. You said there were plenty of black girls in school and I would be safer "courting" one of them. You used words like "fetish" and "experimentation" and "miscegenation." You said Abby Claremont's parents were breaking up over our relationship. You said Abby Claremont didn't know me well enough to love me and only loved the excitement that came with the danger of being with a black boy who drove her father crazy.

I wasn't sure if you were right, but I knew you were in no position to give me advice about relationships given your experiences with Malachi Hunter.

And I told you exactly that.

You beat my body the fuck up again that night. I did not cry. I just watched you swing down until your arms got tired. "What is wrong with you, Kie?" you kept asking. "I know you're a better child than this. What is wrong with you?"

I did not answer because I did not know what was wrong with me.

Abby Claremont and I continued to have sex until near the end of the school year, even though I lied and told you we thought it was safer to just be friends. One weekend, when Malachi Hunter invited you to New Orleans, I told you I was staying at LaThon's house. When you left, I climbed through a window I left open and Abby Claremont and I spent the entire weekend having sex in your bed. We did not use condoms.

That Sunday night, Abby Claremont sat on the edge of your bed talking about cycles of depression in her family, and how our relationship was triggering responses from her parents she never expected. I'd never heard an actual real-life person use the word "depression" before. Scarface was the only artist I knew of who talked about depression. I didn't understand what depression meant, so I told myself it was a made-up white word Scarface stole and it meant "extremely sad."

I asked Abby Claremont if she thought we should stop seeing each other since our relationship was making people in both of our families extremely sad.

"I'm not talking about extreme sadness," she said. "I'm talking about fucking depression."

A few weeks later, you saw me crying in my bedroom after I found out Abby Claremont was considering hooking up with Donnie Gee's cousin, a kid with the highest vertical leap in Jackson. You asked me what was wrong. I told you I was upset that you and my father didn't try harder to make it work.

That made you cry and apologize.

That made me smile and tell more lies.

Other than playing basketball, writing paragraphs, and having sex with Abby Claremont, making you feel what you didn't want to feel when you didn't want to feel it was one of the best feelings in my world. Another incredible feeling was getting away with lying to Abby Claremont after we got back together. I congratulated myself for only kissing and having sexy conversations with other girls, but never having sex with them at Donnie Gee's parties.

Donnie Gee didn't drink our entire junior year because he wanted a basketball scholarship. I lied and told Donnie Gee I wasn't drinking for the same reason. Really, I was afraid I'd hurt myself or someone else if I ever got drunk again.

Before the first party of the year at Donnie Gee's house, Donnie Gee and I bought two forty-ounces of St. Ides. We poured out the malt liquor and filled both empty bottles with off-brand apple juice. We checked each other's noses for floating boogers. We checked our breath for that dragon. We stuffed our mouths with apple Now and Laters and cherry Nerds. When Donnie Gee's doorbell rang, we stumbled around the house, whispering Jodeci lyrics inches under the earlobes of girls who didn't run from us.

Abby Claremont wasn't at the party because she was on punishment for dating me.

About three hours into Donnie Gee's party, Kamala Lackey asked me to follow her into one of the bedrooms. I walked into the dark room behind Kamala Lackey loud-rapping Phife's "Scenario" verse. The room we walked into was the same room where Donnie Gee and I watched Clarence Thomas talk about experiencing a hi-tech lynching when Anita Hill told on him for sexually harassing her. I knew Clarence Thomas was lying because there was no reason in the world for Anita Hill to lie, and because I'd never met one older man who treated women the way he wanted to be treated. Every older man I knew treated every woman he wanted to have sex with like a woman he wanted to have sex with. Clarence Thomas seemed as cowardly as every older man to me.

Once Kamala Lackey and I were both in the room, I complimented her on hair I couldn't see and asked where she got the perfume I couldn't smell. I turned on the light. Kamala Lackey just sat on the edge of Donnie Gee's bed, her fists filled with the comforter, her eyes staring toward the window. I wondered how drunk she was.

"You, you look like Theo Huxtable tonight," I remember Kamala Lackey stuttering as she got up and turned the light off.

I was a sweaty, bald-headed, six-one, 224-pound black boy from Jackson, Mississippi. I owned one pair of jeans, those fake Girbauds that were actually yours, and one decent sweatshirt. Nothing about me looked, moved, or sounded like Theo Huxtable.

When Kamala Lackey asked me if I wanted to see her boobs, I ignored her question, assumed she was definitely drunk, and tried to tell her what I hated about *The Cosby Show*. The sweaters, the corny kids, the problems that weren't problems, the smooth jazz, the manufactured cleanliness, the nonexistent poverty just didn't do it for me. It wasn't only that the Cosbys were never broke, or in need of money, or that none of their black family members and friends were ever in material need of anything important; it was that only in science fiction could a black man doctor who delivered mostly white babies, and a black woman lawyer who worked at a white law firm, come home and never once talk mess about the heartbreaking, violent machinations of white folk at both of their jobs, and the harassing, low-down, predictable advances of men at Clair's office. I remember telling Kamala Lackey how never in the history of real black folk could black life as depicted on *The Cosby Show* ever exist. And it only existed on Cosby's show because Bill Cosby seemed obsessed with how white folk watched black folk watch us watch him.

I didn't exactly say it that way, though.

"Bill Cosby and them be lying too much," is what I said. "That shit fake. You think it's because white folk be watching?"

"Why you still watch that show?" Kamala Lackey asked me. "*A Different World* is way better."

When I got ready to ask her why Denise wasn't on the show anymore, Kamala Lackey asked me again if I wanted to see her boobs.

Of course I wanted to see Kamala Lackey's boobs. Or, of course I wanted Kamala Lackey to think I wanted to see her boobs. Or, of course I wanted to know Kamala Lackey wanted me to see her boobs. When I fake yawned and coughed, Kamala Lackey stood up and asked if I had any more Now and Laters. After I handed her what was left of the pack, she asked if I was really drunk. Before I could lie, Kamala Lackey told me she wasn't drunk either.

She sat on the floor with her back pressed against my knees and made me promise not to tell anyone what she was about to tell me.

I promised.

Thirty minutes later, when Kamala Lackey stopped talking, she also stopped digging her fingers into Donnie Gee's nappy carpet. "You know what I'm trying to say?" she finally asked, and stood in front of the bed. "I feel like I'm dying sometimes."

I said I understood, even though I didn't understand why she was saying any of it to me.

"You gone say something?" I remember her asking. "Go ahead. You know you can talk, right?"

I wanted to tell Kamala Lackey that when I was younger, a few miles from where we were, I got drunk off this box wine you kept in the house. I drank until I was numb because it helped me feel better about what was being done to lips, nipples, necks, thighs, a penis, and a vagina in our house. It felt so scary. I felt so stuck. It all felt like love, too, until it didn't.

Then it felt like dying.

But I didn't say any of that. I told Kamala Lackey thank you for talking to me. I told her I wouldn't tell my boys anything she told me if she didn't tell her girls I was acting drunk. Then we just sat there, wondering who would walk out first.

Like most kids at Donnie Gee's party, I had to sit and listen to hundreds of talks from you and your friends telling me no black hoodies in wrong neighborhoods, no jogging at night, hands in plain sight at all times in public, no intimate relationships with white women, never drive over the speed limit or do those rolling stops at stop signs, always speak the king's English in the presence of white folk, never get outperformed in school or in public by white students, and most important, always remember, no matter what, white folk will do anything to get you.

I listened.

I never heard the words "sexual violence" or "violent sex" or "sexual abuse" from one family member, one teacher, or one preacher but my body knew sexual violence and violent sex were as wrong as anything police or white folk could do to us.

The night Kamala Lackey talked with me, I walked out of Donnie Gee's room the same way I walked in: loudly rapping

Phife's "Scenario" verse, with a turned-up forty in one hand and cupped testicles in the other. Kamala Lackey rolled her eyes at me, shook her head, and turned left down the hall.

I turned right.

When Donnie Gee asked me if I had sex with Kamala Lackey, I smirked and said, "Fool, what you think?" I remember feeling really good about myself because I technically didn't lie to Donnie Gee, and technically didn't touch Kamala Lackey, so I didn't technically cheat on Abby Claremont, the only girl I'd ever kissed.

The night Kamala Lackey told me her secrets, I promised I'd never sexually violate or sexually abuse any woman or girl on earth. The existence of that promise was enough to excuse myself for lying to Abby Claremont and any other girl who wanted to have sex with me. I was sixteen years old. I'd become something far more violent than a Hulk. I was a liar; a cheater; a manipulator; a fat, happysad, bald-headed black boy with a heart murmur; and according to you and the white girl I lied to every day, I was a good dude.

GUMPTION

Near the end of my senior year, I went with you to the house of your mentor, Margaret Walker. I was six-one, 230 pounds. I had $208 in my pocket after delivering phone books in Jackson with LaThon. I thought I was rich.

You'd spent the last few years helping Ms. Walker organize her notes for this massive biography of Aaron Henry. I watched you and Ms. Walker talk about the backlash in Mississippi that led to Kirk Fordice, a reactionary Republican who beat Governor Mabus a few months earlier. Ms. Walker's house was the only house I'd seen in Jackson with more books, folders, African masks, and African lotions than ours. I loved how Ms. Walker seemed nervous and unsure of what she was supposed to be doing next. When I thought she was looking in a cabinet for one of her many folders, without even looking at me she said, "So you are Mary's son, the young writer named after the great Miriam Makeba?"

"I'm not a writer," I told her. "I just write editorials for the school paper. My middle name is Makeba. My first name is Kiese."

"Own our writing, Kiese Makeba," Margaret Walker told me. "Where is your gumption? Own your name. You are a seventeen-year-old black child born in Mississippi. Do you hear me?"

I heard her, but I wasn't sure what she was really saying.

Ms. Walker was even more relentless with the speeches than you were, but not as smooth with the speeches as Grandmama was. She told me to value our communication and own our fight. Our communication, she said, is the mightiest gift passed down by our people. Every word you write and read, every picture you draw, every step you take should be in the service of our people. "Do not be distracted. Be directed. Those people," she said, "they will distract you. They will try to kill you. That's what they do better than most. They distract and they kill. That's why you write for and to our people. Do not be distracted."

I told Ms. Walker I understood her speech, but I was lying. I told her I'd read her poem "For My People" and loved it. I was lying about that, too.

"Have you decided on college? Your mama told me you don't want to go to Jackson State because you don't want her in your business."

"I might be going to Millsaps College," I told her. "They're recruiting me for basketball."

"Oh lord," she said. "I'm talking about revolution and this child is talking about playing some ball at Millsaps."

Ms. Walker marched over to a book on the floor in front of her bookshelf and handed it to me. Half of the book cover was faded pink and half of a woman's face was facing the title, *Cotton Candy on a Rainy Day*.

"If you're going to Millsaps," she said, "I know you will need as much Nikki as you can get."

On the way back home, I read *Cotton Candy on a Rainy Day* cover to cover. When I got to my bedroom, I started reading it again. My favorite part was:

I share with painters the desire
To put a three-dimensional picture
On a One-dimensional surface.

I wrote down what I remembered of Ms. Walker's speech on the last page of the book and I kept coming back to the sentences "They will distract you. They will try to kill you. Do not be distracted. Be directed. Write to and for our people."

I loved those sentences, but I didn't understand the difference between "writing to" and "writing for" anyone. No one ever taught me to write to and for my people. They taught me how to imitate Faulkner and how to write to and for my teachers. And all of my teachers were white. When writing to you, I wrote in the hopes that what I wrote was good enough for me to not get beaten.

I went to the bookshelf and found "For My People." The last words of the last stanza mesmerized and confused me. Margaret Walker wrote:

Let a race of men now rise and take control.

I wanted to write "martial songs" but I didn't understand what a "race of men" looked like, or why Margaret Walker ended the poem hoping a group of men would rise and take control. A group of men hadn't written "For My People." A group of men hadn't told me to write to and for my people. Most groups of men I knew were good at destroying women and girls who would do everything not to destroy them. If a group of men happened to rise and take control, I didn't know where you or Margaret Walker would be when those men got mad at you.

The next day, on April 29, 1992, the night of the Rodney King verdict, you held me in your lap and would not stop rocking for two hours straight. We watched LA burn as cameras showed a white man pulled from a truck getting beat up by black and brown men at an LA intersection.

"I hope you see what they aren't showing," you said. "I want you to write an essay about what white folk feel tonight. I know they're blaming us."

I looked at you like your bread wasn't done because the last thing I cared about was what white folk felt. I'd only been alive seventeen years and I was already tired of paying for white folks' feelings with a generic smile and manufactured excellence they could not give one fuck about. I'd never heard of white folk getting caught and paying for anything they did to us, or stole from us. Didn't matter if it was white police, white teachers, white students, or white randoms. I didn't want to teach white folk not to steal. I didn't want to teach white folk to treat us respectfully. I wanted to fairly fight white folk and I wanted to knock them out. Even more than knocking them out, I wanted to never, ever lose to them again.

I knew there was no way to not lose unless we took back every bit of what had been stolen from us. I wanted all the money, the safety, the education, the healthy choices, and the second chances they stole. If we were to ever get what we were owed, I knew we had to take it all back without getting caught, because no creation on earth was as all-world as white folk at punishing the black whole for the supposed transgressions of one black individual. They were absolute geniuses at inventing new ways for masses of black folk with less to suffer more. Our superpower, I was told since I was a child, was perseverance, the ability to survive no matter how much they took from us. I never understood how surviving was our collective superpower when white folk made sure so many of us didn't survive. And those of us who did survive practiced bending so much that breaking seemed inevitable.

That night when you finally started snoring, I crept into the kitchen, opened the garage, got in your Oldsmobile, put it in neutral, pushed it out of the driveway. I didn't go far, just a mile down the road to the grocery store. I waited in the parking lot for the bread truck to pull up. When the driver went in the store, I got out of the car, snatched as many loaves of wheat bread, white bread, hamburger buns, and cinnamon rolls as I could and took off back to my car. I sped away from the grocery store and drove to a parking lot overlooking the Ross Barnett Reservoir. I ate cinnamon rolls, hamburger buns, and white bread that night until I got the shivers and threw up.

The next morning, I served you some buttered wheat toast for breakfast in bed. You hugged my neck and told me thank you. You told me we would win our fight.

You never asked me where the bread came from.

A week later, I was in Coach Schitzler's twelfth-grade English class. We were supposed to be discussing *The Once and Future King* for the fifth week in a row. I didn't want to discuss *The Once and Future King* anymore so I pulled out *Cotton Candy on a Rainy Day*. When Coach Schitzler saw me reading my book, he said, "Put that black-power mess down, Keece. Pay attention."

I sat in my undersized wooden desk, my fist tucked into my lap, LaThon to my left, Jabari to my right, and began reading stanzas from Nikki Giovanni's book over and over again, loud enough so Coach Schitzler could hear me.

"Look at husky Malcolm X over there," he said. LaThon and everyone else were dying laughing. "Keece X, is that your new name? Well, Keece X, make sure you read that tonight when you see that Abby Claremont Y."

"Oh shit," LaThon said. "He wrong for that."

Coach Schitzler saw I was getting upset. He told me he seriously loved the poem, and suggested I should use it for my final paper. He said he especially loved the end.

I believed him.

I decided to use Nikki Giovanni's book and the work of Assata Shakur for my final for Coach Schitzler's English class. Coach Schitzler, who hated writing comments, gave us recorded comments on these papers incorporating literature and literary devices we read in class, and books we read on our own. He commented on the papers on cassette tapes he handed back near the end of school. I thought he'd be even more generous with all of our papers since he was so late in getting them back to us. I didn't love my paper, because I didn't really want to be writing about *Moby-Dick*, but I thought my next-to-last paragraph was the best writing I'd ever done for Coach Schitzler. It had an allusion to *Moby-Dick*, alliteration, and some commentary on our nation. I tried to write that paragraph for our people, like Margaret Walker asked me to do, even though I had to write it to Coach Schitzler because he was grading me.

Though I agree with Assata Shakur that a "lost ship, steered by tired, seasick sailors, can still be guided home to port," I know tired, seasick American sailors and their families have absolutely no chance at health and dignified lives, unless some Americans first accept

their responsibility, and work to calm the bruising bru-
tality of our national sea.

I took the tape home, and just as I had with tapes I dubbed
from LaThon, I put the tape in the little radio next to my bed.

"Keece Lay-moon," the tape began. Ever since Coach
Schitzler learned I was in a relationship with Abby Claremont, he said my name like I was some scraggly French dude
he paid to cut his yard.

"Keece," he said again. "I want to say first that you need
to watch your weight if you want to play ball in college. You
getting close to two-forty and there's no way you can play
even Division Three ball at that weight. You a shooting guard
on the next level, not a power forward. The problem with this
paper is it relies on faulty logic." I could hear him flipping the
pages. "Faulty logic on page three. Faulty logic on page four.
The paper is all just a mess of faulty logic. I see glimpses of
your argumentative mind, but you undermine it with faulty
logic. Maybe you should get your mommy to help you with
papers for class like she does with your newspaper editorials."

Coach Schitzler saw everything as a quest, and every black
boy as his potential hero. He saw black and white girls as dar-
lings, damsels, or damned. I wanted him to see me as the young
black Mississippi hero jousting with words, paragraphs, and
punctuation. I wanted him to tell me how my writing had the
potential to be some of the best writing to come out of Mississippi, or Jackson, or at least our high school.

The night I listened to Coach Schitzler's tape, you kept
coming into my room, asking me why I was crying. I told you
I didn't really know.

"You're lying to me, Kie," you said. "Tell me the truth."

I rolled my eyes, handed you the essay, and played the tape for you.

"Fuck him," you said after listening to a minute of Coach Schitzler's response. "Do you hear me? Do not internalize their shit. I'm going to school with you tomorrow to put my whole foot off in that man's ass."

I made you promise you wouldn't embarrass me by coming to school. You promised and sat next to me. You took my paper smudged with tears and you read it out loud. You told me what worked in the essay, and what didn't work. You asked me questions about word choice, pacing, and something you called political symbolism. You asked me what I was really trying to say with the essay and suggested I start with saying exactly that. You challenged me to use the rest of the essay to discover ideas and questions I didn't already know and feel. "A good question anchored in real curiosity is much more important than a cliché or forced metaphor," you told me.

By the end of the night, you helped me revise the essay into a piece I was proud of, even though Coach Schitzler had already given the paper a C. I understood for the first time that day how Coach Schitzler, just like most of the grown black men I knew, wanted to set people's brains on fire before situating himself as the only one who could calm the blaze. He wanted us to praise him for his tough love, which was really a way of encouraging students to thank him for not hurting us as much as he could.

"Internalizing their abusive bullshit will make you crazy, Kie," you said before you went to your bedroom. "I love you so much and I hate seeing you hurt."

I believed you.

The next day when I asked Coach Schitzler to explain himself, he said everything he had to say was on the tape. I said I didn't understand the tape and that you read my essays but never wrote the essays for me.

"She's a teacher," I told him. "But she don't write my papers."

"You looking like you ready to jump," Coach Schitzler said in front of the class. His gumption surprised me. He stepped from behind his desk. "If you jump at me like you grown, don't be mad if you get knocked upside the head like you grown."

I balled up my fists.

When Coach Schitzler got shoulder to shoulder with me, I didn't say anything. I leaned most of my weight on his shoulder and hoped to God he swung, so I could cave in his chest.

He backed up and stepped behind his desk.

"You know your problem?" he asked, and pointed at me. "Besides arrogance and that silly argumentative mind, your problem, Keece Lay-moon, is that you ain't got no daddy at home."

Ms. Andrews, LaThon, and two other teachers had to peel me off Coach Schitzler that day because of what he said about you. I didn't tell you what he said because I knew I'd have to peel you off him, too.

I ended Schitzler's English class with the lowest D you could earn without failing. Thankfully, I won a few awards from the Mississippi Scholastic Press Association in high school, got recruited to play basketball, and did well enough on the ACT to get into Millsaps.

But my GPA was shameful.

With two weeks of school left, I wrote an essay for our

paper about how the mostly black graduates of St. Joseph deserved so much more than having our graduation speaker be the reactionary Republican governor of our state, Kirk Fordice. When the school invited Governor Fordice anyway, I told LaThon, you, and my teachers I wasn't going to graduation. No one believed me.

I didn't go to graduation.

That decision, as much as any paragraph I'd written, was when I became a writer. And it wasn't because I didn't attend graduation. It was because the night before graduation, you made me write through all the reasons I didn't want to attend graduation. The whole truth was that I felt trunk-loads of shame for graduating five places from the bottom of my class when I easily could have been near the top if I would have applied myself and stopped trying to punish both of us.

All my friends and family patted me on my back for having the gumption to skip graduation, except you and Grandmama. I sat in Grandmama's dining room with both of you, eating my second plate of macaroni and cheese while LaThon and the rest of my classmates were walking across that stage in front of Kirk Fordice and Coach Schitzler.

When I reached for a third serving of macaroni and cheese, you told Grandmama I'd had enough.

"How you know I had enough if I still want more?" I asked you.

"Get up from the table," you said. "Go outside and get a grip."

I rolled my eyes, sucked my teeth, and went out on Grandmama's porch.

"You wanna know the truth?" Grandmama said while we sat out on the porch. "After all them ass whuppings and child support payments that ain't never come, I don't reckon you wanted your daddy or your mama taking no joy in watching you walk across the stage. I don't much blame you for it neither, Kie. But the problem is you hurting yourself by trying to let folk know they hurt you. God gives us five senses for a reason. You hear me? Use them. Stop hunting for distractions. Stop taking your own legs out. It's enough mess out there trying to beat us down without you helping. I reckon your mama the least of your troubles. Did you at least tell your teachers in that schoolhouse thank you?"

I sat there thinking about all the teachers I had from first through twelfth grade. I'd gone to majority black schools all but that one year at St. Richard and that one year at DeMatha. Ms. Arnold, my fourth-grade teacher, was the only black teacher I had. Ms. Raphael, who taught us at Holy Family in sixth and seventh grade, loved us so much that LaThon and I once made the mistake of calling her Mama. The rest of my teachers maybe did the best they could, but they just needed a lot of help making their best better. There were so many things we needed in those classrooms, in our city, in our state, in our country that our teachers could have provided if they would have gone home and really done their homework. They never once said the words: "economic inequality," "housing discrimination," "sexual violence," "mass incarceration," "homophobia," "empire," "mass eviction," "post traumatic stress disorder," "white supremacy," "patriarchy," "neo-confederacy," "mental health," or "parental abuse," yet every student and teacher at that school lived in a world shaped by those words.

I loved all my teachers, and I wanted all my teachers to love us. I knew they weren't being paid right. I knew they were expected to do work they were unprepared to start or

finish. But I felt like we spent much of our time teaching them how to respect where we'd been, and they spent much of their time punishing us for teaching them how we deserved to be treated.

Later that summer, I saw LaThon before he left for the University of Alabama. We would always be friends, but we'd stopped taking care of each other when I started seeing Abby Claremont. LaThon told me he got in some trouble at Freaknik and needed Malachi Hunter to connect him with a lawyer who could help get a case thrown out before his school heard about it. I told him I didn't really talk with Malachi Hunter at all anymore, and even if I did, Malachi Hunter might have been in some legal trouble of his own.

"You the only one of us who ain't caught up with the police," he said. "And you the craziest one of all of us."

"I ain't crazy, not like that."

"Bruh," he said and looked at me without blinking. "Come on, bruh. You ain't crazy like that? Who you think you talking to? Ever since fourth grade, who got kicked out of school more than you? Who was fucking around with a white girl knowing his mama did not play? Who was steady telling these white folk the truth to they face? Who gave the whole bus a speech about fucking without condoms after Magic got HIV? Who was talking shit to the police like they weren't police since we were like twelve years old? You the only person I know who will do and say anything anywhere anytime. Swear to God, you the only person I know who ain't scared of nothing we supposed to be scared of. But I'm like how this nigga got all that gumption, and somehow, he ain't never even been arrested?"

"Not yet."

"You still don't drank or smoke weed?"

"Not yet."

"Not yet?" LaThon mocked me. "If you ain't smoke yet, you ain't never gone smoke. You think it's 'cause your mama beat the tar out of your ass all the time?"

I dapped LaThon up and hugged him. "Nah," I said. "I don't think it's 'cause my mama beat the tar out my ass. We all scared of something."

"I'm just playing," he said. "Quit being sensitive. I can't believe you staying in Jackson and going to that white-ass private school. You forgot how meager it was the last time we went to one of they schools in eighth grade?"

"I love you, bruh," I told him for the first time in our lives. "Don't forget about your boys when you in engineering school."

"I love you, too, bruh. Don't forget about your boys when you get kicked out of that private white school."

"Ain't nobody getting kicked out of college," I told him. "It's still that black abundance, right?"

"You already know," LaThon said. "All day. Every day. And they still don't even know."

III.

HOME WORKED.

FANTASTIC

You sat in the driver's seat singing the wrong lyrics to Mary J. Blige's "Real Love" while I rode shotgun wishing you would drive faster. We were headed to the airport. You'd been awarded another postdoc. This one was at Harvard University for the entire academic year. I was eighteen years old, 242 pounds. I had $175 to my name.

"Do you try to sing the lyrics wrong every time?" I asked you.

"Sometimes."

We didn't say another word until we were in front of your departure gate. "I think we need this time away," you said. "Maybe I'll worry less about you if I know I can't control anything you do."

"Maybe."

"I know," you said. "I know."

I asked you if I could take some books from the house to have in my dorm room. You reached up, pulled on my neck, and kissed me on the top of the head. I pulled away. "Maybe the books will protect you," you said. "Take all the books you need. And don't fight when you're angry. Think when you're angry. Write when you're angry. Read when you're angry. Don't let those people shoot you out of the sky while I'm gone." I rolled my eyes and sucked hard on my teeth as

119

you walked to the end of the line. "Don't be good," you said across the space between us. "Be perfect. Be fantastic."

You smiled. I smiled.

You waved. I waved.

You fake yawned. I fake yawned.

You disappeared. I was free.

I wanted you to be safe in Boston and get your work done. I wanted you to finally find healthy, affirming love and all that stuff they sang about on the adult contemporary radio stations. I also didn't want you to ever come back to Mississippi if I was there.

Instead of driving back to Millsaps, I went to the Waffle House across from the Coliseum, right next to the Dunkin' Donuts, and ordered the all-you-can-eat special on the left side of the menu. I'd never driven myself to a restaurant. Sitting alone and ordering a waffle, an omelet, hash browns, cheese grits, a patty melt, and another waffle with pecans made me feel grown. I cleaned all my plates, walked next door, ordered a dozen donuts from Dunkin' Donuts without wondering or caring how the caked-up glaze on my face looked to anyone.

I felt so free.

The next day, all the first- and second-year black boys gathered in Clinton Mayes's room. We all liked each other on Friday night when no one was drinking. We all loved each other Saturday night when nearly everyone was drunk.

I hadn't had a drink in seven years because I was afraid I'd shoot myself or someone else. But I smiled a lot, and I nodded, and I listened, and I blinked my big red eyes really slowly, and said "that's funny to me" every eight minutes. That, and the fact I was from Jackson, was enough to make folk think I was drunk and high.

I heard the sentence "We gone make it" more than thirty-four times that weekend. The sentence was always followed by a hug, a "you already know," or an offering of a peppermint from this hovering long-neck senior named Myles.

I learned to say "You already know" and "We gone make it" that weekend, too, but I didn't understand why we wouldn't make it. Most of us made it through high school in Mississippi. At Millsaps, we were only reading books. We were only writing papers. We were only taking tests. The students surrounding us were only white, and all of us were Mississippi, black, and abundant. That meant we were the kinfolk of Fannie Lou Hamer, Ida B. Wells, and Medgar Evers. I assumed we were wittier, tougher, and more imaginative than white students, administrators, and faculty because we had to be.

I told a super-duper senior from Winona named Ray Gunn he looked like a bootleg Stokely Carmichael. "You mean, Kwame Ture old ass looked like me when he was young," he said.

I told Gunn I assumed the teachers at Saps would do everything possible, in and out of the classroom, to make sure all of us did far more than make it. Even though Ray Gunn just looked at me and blinked, we got along well the first day we met because he was shameless and loved trying to invent slang that never stuck. "These Saps teachers," he said, "they gives no fuck about dumb black blasters like us when we leave that classroom. You ain't special. I ain't special. Not to them. Or you way too special because they think you an exception to the race. You'll see. You better practice saying words like 'fantastic' in the mirror. Saps is known for making dumb blasters forget who they wanted to be."

There weren't many black boys at Millsaps, but nearly all of us were football and basketball recruits from Mississippi. Ray Gunn told me when most of the black boys in his class lost their eligibility, they went back home, or went to work somewhere, and never graduated. "All that," he said, "and them damn oral and written comps be fucking up our flow. Flow-fuckers. They be thinning out dumb blasters faster than you think."

The black girls I met that first weekend were not recruited to play a sport, but like us, they hadn't been around this many white folk with money before either. Most of them said they wanted to be doctors, accountants, or lawyers. This freshly dressed bowlegged girl named Nzola Johnston made the whole room fall out laughing when she called herself "fake-ass Denise Huxtable at night" and a "fake-ass Claire Huxtable during the day." Nzola told all the girls, in front of all the boys, that they had to look out for themselves because black women couldn't count on these white folk or "those niggas over there" to look out for them.

When I wasn't in class, in the cafeteria, playing basketball, or driving to get food, I spent most of my first semester in my room writing parts of essays I hoped to plug into paper assignments. I acted the part of a smart black boy from Mississippi, even though it was harder for me to dress the part. I used all my work-study money to buy sweet potato pies and gas instead of clothes that fit. After a month in school, the one pair of khakis I liked to wear couldn't fit around the bottom of my ass.

The first few weeks of school, I was asked by security to show my ID inside my room a few times and I was accused of plagiarism for using the word "ambivalent" in an English class. I wanted to tell the teacher who accused me how I never even used a thesaurus when writing because I thought that was cheating. Immediately after the plagiarism accusation, I started bringing five books to all my classes. Usually, the books had nothing to do with the class I was taking. I sometimes stacked the books on my desk. Sometimes I slowly brought them out one at a time, and even slower, I placed them back in my briefcase, letting the white students and professor know I'd read more than they would.

In class, I only spoke when I could be an articulate defender of black people. I didn't use the classroom to ask questions. I didn't use the classroom to make ungrounded claims. There was too much at stake to ask questions, to be dumb, to be a curious student, in front of a room of white folk who assumed all black folk were intellectually less than. For the first time in my life, the classroom scared me. And when I was scared, I ran to cakes, because cakes felt safe, private, and celebratory.

Cakes never fought back.

By the time I met Nzola Johnston again, my thighs rubbed raw and newer stretch marks streaked across my belly. When Nzola walked past my table at the grill one Wednesday night, I was halfway through three big greasy pieces of Red Velvet cake and was reading a book by Derrick Bell called *Faces at the Bottom of the Well.*

Nzola Johnston walked past my table on the way out, rocking the bushiest eyebrows and deepest frown lines of anyone I've ever met other than Grandmama. She dressed like she worked at the Gap and listened to A Tribe Called Quest 24/7, but she talked like she was bored to death of dudes in Jackson who worked at the Gap and listened to A Tribe Called Quest 24/7.

"You like to read, huh?" she asked. I didn't say anything. I just nodded up and down in slo-mo. "Oh, okay," she said. "I'm

Kenyatta's roommate, Nzola. She said you like Digable Planets and be making all kinds of sense in liberal studies class."

"That's what's up," I said. "I know who you are. We already met."

"Just because you were in a room looking at my ass does not mean we met. What's your name mean?"

"Joy," I told her. "In Kikongo, it means joy. My father was in Zaire when I was born. What about Nzola?"

"If you want to know, you'll find out. I'll definitely see you later, Kiese."

I decided that night I was going to come to the Grill every day of the week with a different book, hoping Nzola Johnston would see me reading. I stayed in the library that night trying to find what Nzola meant. When I couldn't find it, the librarian told me I should try the Internet.

"The what?" I asked her.

"Never mind," she said. "I'll look around and see what I can find for you."

Six nights after Nzola Johnston said she would definitely see me later, I watched her say "I'll definitely see you later" to two black seniors sweating her way too hard. After she walked out of the Grill, and they walked out after her, Nzola came back.

"You running away from something," she said during our first conversation. "I am, too. I don't know what I'm running from but I'm definitely running. What about you?"

"What about me?"

"You running from something," she said again. "Or you wouldn't be here tonight hoping I showed up." Before I could say anything, Nzola kept talking. She said she watched you doing election analysis on WJTV for years. She called you one of her heroes, and asked me what life was like growing up in the house of such a strong, brilliant black woman. I started to answer when she said, "These white girls are so trifling. A few of them act like they got some sense. Most of them, not a drop of sense. Not one drop. But they got all the money. It's so annoying. What about you?"

"What about me?"

"The money stuff doesn't get on your nerves?"

I didn't want the white folk at Millsaps or Nzola to know I just got a bank account and only had thirty-seven dollars in it. I didn't want them to know thirty-seven dollars was a lot of disposable income to everyone in our family near the third week of every month.

"They do them," I said. "We do us. My money is good so I'm good. Is it weird having a name that means 'love'?"

"Your money that good?" she asked, ignoring my game. "Or you that free? Because I'm trying be free. You think you the shit because you found out what my name means?"

"Yup," I said. "I think I'm the shit because I found out what your name means." I called Nzola an ol' fake-ass Angela Davis and told her I was trying to be free, too, and it helped that my money was already good. She asked me why I always talked about my money being good. I laughed and laughed and laughed until I didn't.

Nzola and I met at the Grill over greasy pieces of Red Velvet cake five days in a row. The next week, I bought her the new Digable Planets tape and took her out to the Chinese buffet every day for lunch or dinner. I bounced two checks and exceeded the limit on my new credit card the following week. The week after Nzola, Ray Gunn, and I were falsely accused of plagiarizing a paper in separate English classes, I bounced two more checks on an Izod rugby shirt.

Every waking moment on that campus was filled with my trying to misdirect people from seeing who I really was. Misdirection was fun, but it was also exhausting. I wasn't sure who I really was, but I understood where I was. I was right in the middle of Jackson, my city, but I was so far from home.

When I was admitted into Millsaps, I knew on one side of the school was the neighborhood of Belhaven, where wealthy white liberals who hadn't flown to Madison and Rankin lived. On the other side of the college was a poor black neighborhood called the North End. I knew the gates facing the North End were always bolted shut, and the gates facing Belhaven were always open, always welcoming. I knew that white boys at my majority black high school got punched in their mouths repeatedly for wearing Confederate flags on their shirts or talking mess about the Old South. I knew at Millsaps that those shirts were as common as fake Polos and Izods.

One semester into school, and I now knew most of the groundskeepers were black men. I knew most of the cafeteria workers and folk who cleaned the dorms were black women. I knew the fraternities and sororities spent Thursday, Friday, and Saturday out of their minds, breaking things that shouldn't be broken. I knew dorms, classrooms, offices, paths, and parties were filled with white students, faculty, and administrators saying in their own way that our presence at their school was proof they were innocent, and could never be racist. I knew, after a semester at Millsaps, books couldn't save me from a college, classes, a library, dorms, and a cafeteria that belonged to wealthy white folk. I never expected to have that feeling right in the middle of my city.

Two weeks later, Nzola and I were in her room, kissing

each other's necks like it was going out of style while her roommate slept. I saw pictures of Nzola's boyfriend's face down under her bed next to these blue paintings and brown chicken-wire sculptures. Nzola's boyfriend's jawline was so pronounced. He looked like Lance, one of Theo's friends from *The Cosby Show*.

Nzola whispered she wanted us to be like Bill and Hillary Clinton except we'd actually love black folk and not just what black folk did for us.

"Cool," I said, and kissed her forehead. "Your boyfriend probably won't like you being married to me, though."

"Neither will your white girlfriend," she said. I hadn't told her about my relationship with Abby Claremont, but someone else had.

"What white girlfriend?"

"Wow," Nzola said. "You didn't use to mess with a white girl? Niggas these days love acting like niggas these days."

Three weeks later, right before Thanksgiving break, Nzola and I were on a stage after midnight in the academic complex doing the heaviest petting I'd ever done. Nzola told me she loved my bottom lip and never wanted to stop kissing me.

I didn't believe her.

She asked if we should go somewhere private because there were hidden cameras on campus watching every move we made. We headed back to her room since Kenyatta was gone for the weekend. Nzola handed me a condom while we were on the floor.

"What's your boyfriend's name?" I asked her. "He's way older than us and he's a doctor, right?"

"He's just a good friend," she said. "And yeah, he's a doctor. He's twenty-seven."

"What's your twenty-seven-year-old good friend the doctor's name?"

"His name is James."

"How you end up with a Golden Grahams–type dude with a basic-ass name like Dr. James?" I asked her.

"What's your girlfriend's name? Molly, right? Or something like Claire," she said. "I don't care what that white skeezer's name is. I wanna ask you something."

"What?"

"I want you to tell me what being with me makes you feel."

"For real?"

"Yeah," she said. "For real. Like what do your insides feel when you're around me?"

"Heavy," I told her.

"Heavy like deep?"

"Maybe a little, but more heavy like huge. Heavy like dumb fat. What about you?"

"But heavy and huge and dumb fat are three completely different things," she said.

"You think so?"

"I'm small but I know I'm heavy. What about you?"

Nzola's baggy clothes and full cheeks cloaked a tiny frame. She wasn't just tiny compared to me, or tiny compared to Abby Claremont; she was tiny compared to every woman who'd ever kissed me. "You asked me and I told you. You can't tell I gained like forty pounds since school started."

"I can't tell," she said.

"Why you lying?"

"I'm not lying. I can't tell. But even if I could tell, so what?"

I told Nzola I had to go back to my dorm and finish a

paper. She asked if she could come with me. The paper was due in the morning, I told her, and it was hard for me to concentrate if I was working next to someone.

"Other people's breathing throws off your thinking, Kiese?"

"I mean, kinda, but more like . . ."

"You are some kind of strange-ass dude, Kiese Laymon," she said. "Even when I know you're lying to me, I just feel crazy sorry for you."

"Why?"

"Because I can just tell you'll never let me carry' what you're hiding."

I thought about what Nzola said, but I didn't think about what I was hiding. I hadn't thought about what I was hiding the whole time I'd been at Millsaps. "You won't let me hold what you're hiding, either. And it's obvious you're hiding just as much as me."

"Yep. You're right," she said. "That's different. I know y'all. Y'all love to see us break."

"I'm not trying to see you break, though."

"If you want me to believe you when you're lying," she said, "then you want to see me break."

Nzola invited me to her house for Thanksgiving, but I didn't go because her stepmother was always commenting on Nzola's weight and how she wanted "a fine, handsome, together brother" for her stepdaughter. I'd been treated like a man in and out of our house for about a decade. But I was also forever the kind of black boy who could never really be a fine, handsome, together brother because I was too husky to be fine and too dusty to be together.

Even though the dorms were closed, I spent Thursday

through Sunday in the student lounge eating everything I could afford off the ninety-nine-cent menu at Wendy's. When all my Wendy's was gone, I broke into vending machines on campus. I stole their Moon Pies, Hot Fries, Twix, and Grandma's Vanilla Sandwich Cremes. I kicked my feet up on their couch and watched *The Arsenio Hall Show* on their television. Before falling asleep, I started reading a book I checked out of their library by Toni Cade Bambara. The book was called *Gorilla, My Love*.

It does no good to write autobiographical fiction cause the minute the book hits the stand here comes your mama screamin how could you and sighin death where is thy sting and she snatches you up out your bed to grill you about what was going down back there in Brooklyn when she was working three jobs and trying to improve the quality of your life and come to find on page 42 that you were messin around with that nasty boy up the block and breaks into sobs and quite naturally your family strolls in all sleepy-eyed to catch the floor show at 5:00 A.M. but as far as your mama is concerned, it is nineteen-forty-and-something and you ain't too grown to have your ass whupped.

The first sentence of the book showed me first sentences could be roller coasters designed especially for us. I read it again. Then I wrote it. Bambara took what Welty did best and created worlds where no one was sheltered, cloistered, or white, but everyone—in some form or fashion—was weird, wonderful, slightly wack, and all the way black. Blackness, in all its boredom and boom, was the historical and imaginative context in Bambara's work. I wanted to be that kind of free, on and off the page. I wanted to write something someday with that kind of first sentence and I wanted that kind of first sentence to be written to me every day for the rest of my life.

I still wrote every night and revised every morning, but practicing crafting formidable sentences just made me a formidable sentence writer. The other part of writing required something more than just practice, something more than reading, too. It required loads of unsentimental explorations of black love. It required an acceptance of our strange. And mostly, it required a commitment to new structures, not reformation. I'd spent eighteen years reading the work of supposed excellent sentence-writers who did not love, or really see us. Many wrote for us, without writing to us. After reading Bambara, I wondered for the first time how great an American sentence, paragraph, or book could be if it wasn't, at least partially, written to and for black Americans in the Deep South.

A few days before winter break, Nzola invited me to the Grill to eat greasy pieces of Red Velvet cake. I brought *Gorilla, My Love* because I wanted to see her face when she read the first sentence. "So James asked me to visit him for Christmas break," she said while we were eating.

"That's cool," I told her, and put the book back in my book bag. "Tell Dr. Rick James hey for me."

"I don't want to go, Kiese," she said.

"For real? What would Bill Clinton do?"

"He would lie, and fuck whoever he wants," Nzola said without cracking a smile. "Then he'd lie again." I told her I'd been working on an essay about Bill Clinton. "That's all you have to say?" she asked, and hugged my neck. "That's really all you have to say?"

"Yup."

"I guess I'll see you later. Good luck with your essay. Send it to me if you want. I hope you have a fantastic break."

Nzola never used "fantastic" in conversation with me before that day, the day we broke up without ever really going together. No black person I knew ever used "fantastic" before that day other than you and Ray Gunn when he was warning me.

That night, I went searching through all the garbage cans in my dorm looking for uneaten slices of pizza. On the first and second floor alone, I found enough to make an entire eight-slice pie. I stacked the slices one on top of another and placed them on a paper towel. I started to turn on the microwave in the dorm kitchen when Ray Gunn tapped me on my shoulder.

"Fuck is you doing?" he asked.

I told him Nzola used "fantastic" when she said bye to me.

"Oh, it's a wrap then," he said, throwing my pizza in the garbage, slice by slice. "Nigga, you depressed?"

"What you mean?"

"I mean what I said. You depressed, ain't you?" Ray Gunn started telling me about his ninth semester at Millsaps when a teacher suggested he see a psychiatrist. "I was feeling like you look. Gaining weight and shit. I talked to the dude about stuff like suicide and psychosis. All of a sudden, this white nigga prescribing me with antidepressants."

"Did they work?"

"That shit had me feeling so white, blaster."

"White how?"

"Just white," he said. "Not too high. Not too low. You know when blasters say 'I don't give a fuck'? Nobody who say 'I don't give a fuck' has ever been on antidepressants. Antidepressants make you give nan fuck about nothing. I felt so white." I was bent over dying laughing. "I'm serious. I bullshit you not. If you go, don't go to a psychiatrist. Go to a psychologist."

"What's the difference?"

"The difference is one will listen to you, and try to blame your mama, and maybe your daddy, and one will give you pills to make yo big ass feel white."

"Nah," I told him. "I'm good."

"How you good? You had a fine bowlegged genius sweating your fat ass, and you fucked around and got her using 'fantastic' when she say bye to you. You the smartest dumb blaster I met at Saps, but you might be the saddest dumb blaster to ever enroll in the twelve semesters I been here. Don't eat when you sad, though. I'm serious. Don't eat or drank or gamble when you sad. Pray. Or talk to me. Or exercise. Or just go to bed. You letting all this shit kill you. That's exactly what they want," Ray Gunn said. "Trust me. I been there. You my boy, but you might wanna think about transferring. Ain't nothing fantastic about where you at. Switch that shit up. Be a switch hitter."

"A switch hitter? That's your new shit. You know that already means something else, right?"

"I know what they say it mean, but when I say it, I mean what I mean," he said. "You see how I be hitting them switches in my Impala? You see how I'm steady switching up my styles? Be like me, dumb blaster. Be a switch hitter."

I dapped Ray Gunn up and told him I had no idea what he was talking about before walking him to his Impala.

"Bruh, I finally understand you," I told him. "You a forever nineties-type nigga. Like even in the seventies, you were a nineties-type nigga and even in the two thousands you still gonna be a nineties-type nigga."

"You just realizing that, dumb blaster?"

"Yeah, I'm just realizing that," I told him. "On the serious tip, thanks for telling me about your experience with those pills. For real. I appreciate that."

When I made it back to my room, I wanted the greasy pizza Ray Gunn threw in the garbage. I thought writing might distract my appetite, so I got my notebook and wrote through why Ray Gunn saying antidepressants made him feel white was so funny.

I read.

I looked out of the window.

I felt the painted cement wall behind my head.

I read.

I looked out of the window.

I wrote.

An hour later, I walked back down to the kitchen, dug six of the eight slices out of the garbage, ran warm water on them, picked off the pepperoni, and warmed up my second dinner.

I didn't feel depressed. I didn't feel white. I felt so free. I felt so fantastic.

DISASTER

When you came home for your Christmas break, you looked at me, shook your head, and asked, "What are you doing to yourself?"

You made me get on the scale in front of you.

256.

264.

269.

272.

275.

287.

296.

I asked you to leave, then took all my clothes off and tip-toed on the scale again.

293.

In one semester, three and a half months, I gained over fifty pounds. The only good thing about the weight was you seemed disgusted when I acted like I didn't care.

The next day when I came home from selling Cutco knives, you were in your room. "Why do you say that?" I heard you ask someone on the phone that night. "I will tell him when I have to. I don't have to now. I'll come see you when I can."

I didn't know whom you were talking to, but I could tell by the whispery, welcoming tone it wasn't Malachi Hunter. Even though Malachi Hunter had a new baby with another woman, he wouldn't leave you alone. It's not so much he wanted you back; it's that he didn't want you to want anyone else. Whenever he invited himself over, you asked me not to leave the house. As soon as his car pulled into the driveway, I went under your pillow, got your gun, and put it in my pocket.

Malachi Hunter came into my room without knocking that night you were whispering on the phone. I had the gun underneath the covers, between my thighs. He didn't say hey or how you doing or what's up. "The white man, he'll get you one way or another," he said. "You can't be a black scholar and be free unless you independently wealthy. You can't be independently wealthy and be the white man's labor. Let's say your mama needs to go to the conference for revolutionaries in Nairobi, as smart as she is, does she have the money to go?"

"There's a conference for revolutionaries in Nairobi?"

"Laymon," he said, "catch up. You supposed to be a writer. Use your imagination. Goddamn."

You appeared in my doorway and told him he needed to leave. Y'all didn't fight. Y'all didn't argue. Malachi Hunter laughed in your face and kept talking like you weren't there. "She still ain't free, Laymon," he said. "She the smartest woman in the world, but she not free. It's too many cheese-eating niggas in this house who think free and black are oxymorons. I'm allergic to houses like this. I'm gone, Laymon."

I followed Malachi Hunter out the front door. I stayed in the driveway until I couldn't see the lights of his Jaguar anymore.

Later on that night, you knocked on my bedroom door. I was working on a satirical essay about Millsaps College filled with something I called "Laymon's terms."

"Can I come in, Kie?"

I put my notebook down and didn't say a word. You sat on the edge of the bed just looking at the carpet. You wanted me to ask you a question but I didn't have anything to ask other than "What's wrong?"

"I don't know, Kie," you said. "Sometimes I think I go from one disaster to another."

"But why?" I asked you.

"Why what?"

"Why do you go from one disaster to another?"

"I think part of me feels most calm during those really quick destructive storms."

"But maybe you'd feel even more calm during calm."

"Yeah," you said. "I think you're right. I averted at least one disaster. I stopped seeing Malachi when you were in high school because I knew our relationship was toxic for you. Anyway, I wrote my last check today. Do you have forty dollars I could use until the rest of my checks come?"

I didn't say a word. I just blinked, listened to what I thought was bullshit, and eventually gave you what you came to my room for: a long hug, forty dollars, and the promise I would always love you no matter how many disasters you walked into. I didn't know the man you were talking to on the phone, but I hoped with every cell in my body that if he was a disaster, y'all could create something a lot less disastrous than what you and Malachi Hunter created.

That night, I started rereading *Black Boy*. Reading the book at Millsaps felt like a call to arms. Reading the book in my bed, a few feet from your room, in our house, felt like a warm whisper. Richard Wright wrote about disasters and he let the reader know that there wasn't one disaster in America that started the day everything fell apart. I wanted to write

137

like Wright far more than I wanted to write like Faulkner, but I didn't really want to write like Wright at all. I wanted to fight like Wright. I wanted to craft sentences that styled on white folk, and dared them to do anything about the styling they'd just witnessed. I understood why Wright left Jackson, left Mississippi, left the Deep South, and ultimately left the nation. But I kept thinking about how Grandmama didn't leave when she could. I thought about how you left and chose to come back. I thought about how I chose to stay. I wondered if the world would have ever read Wright had he not left Mississippi. I wondered if black children born in Mississippi after Wright would have laughed, or smiled more at his sentences if he imagined Mississippi as home. I wondered if he thought he'd come back home soon the day he left for Chicago.

The next day, the lights in the house were off. Like always, you said there must be a problem with all the lights in the neighborhood. Before leaving for the airport back to Harvard, you checked the mail. A Millsaps College report card was in that box on top of a stack of bills you refused to bring in the house.

I had not been a perfect student.

I stood in front of the bookcase waiting for you. You marched into your room, went in the closet, and came out with a belt. You brought one lash down across my shoulder. You brought another lash down across the front of my stomach. I didn't move. You went on and on about ruining the only chance I had to get free.

I grabbed the belt, snatched it from your hand, and threw it against the bookcase. You looked at me for the first time in my life the same way you looked at Malachi Hunter when he was angry. I knew your body was afraid of mine. You knew, for the first time in our lives, my body was not afraid of yours.

Malachi Hunter was outside the house, blowing his horn.

Before walking out of the house, you said I was the saddest, most self-destructive person you'd ever met. I told you if you wanted me to listen to anything you had to say, you needed to learn to pay your damn light bill and stop riding in cars with disasters.

We were both telling the truth.

We were both lying.

We were both telling the truth.

ALREADY

I went to the Grill and waited for Nzola Johnston for two weeks. She never showed up. Ray Gunn told me he'd seen her walking around campus with an older yellow-brown brother who kept his beard extra crispy. He said the yellow-brown dude was pigeon-toed and walked around with a red briefcase. He was supposedly narrow through the hips but his forearms were on swole.

"Not Popeye forearms," Ray Gunn said, "but similar to Brutus, I swear to God."

"You act like the dude carried his own sunset, Gunn."

"This blaster *was* a sunset," he said. "It ain't in my nature to want to be another blaster, but this blaster was perfect."

"How you know he perfect just from looking at him?"

"I mean, wait until you see him. He definitely lifting heavy and doing all the cardio. I mean . . ."

"I hear you," I told him. "You can be quiet now. That blaster stuff, I don't think it's catching on. It's been like almost a year. You the only one who uses it."

Gunn just looked at me, acted like he was fixing his left contact. "Like I was saying," he finally said, "the dumb blaster your fine-ass ex was with had arms similar to Brutus."

I never went to professors' office hours, and rarely spoke in any of my classes anymore. I read all the books I was assigned for Latin, philosophy, and English. I did my papers

for all my classes, but the only class I attended and partici-
pated in regularly was a class called "Introduction to Wom-
en's Studies." I read everything for the class twice, arrived
early, and stayed late because the class gave me a new vocabulary to make sense of what I saw growing up. Before the
class, I knew men, regardless of race, had the power to abuse
in ways women didn't. I knew the power to abuse destroyed
the interiors of men as much as it destroyed the interiors and
exteriors of women.

I now knew what "patriarchy" was. I could define "com-
pulsory heterosexuality." I could explain "intersectionality" to
Ray Gunn. I understood gender was a construction and there
were folk on earth who were transgender and gender-fluid. I
went to abortion-clinic defenses. I marched in safer-sex ral-
lies. I made photocopies of my bell hooks essays and gave
them to my friends. I had new lenses and frames to see the
world. I called those new lenses and frames "black feminist,"
but I didn't really have the will to publicly or privately reckon
with what living my life as a black feminist meant.

Reckon or not, the white women in women's studies class
treated me like I was the most liberated of good dudes. A
few of them asked to go for long walks so we could talk
about the reading. If I wasn't so fat, I would have gone, but
I hated sweating and breathing loud around women I didn't
know. I spent most of my days wondering what Nzola was
feeling, eating all the leftover pizza I could find, touching my
body gently in the dark, rereading Lucille Clifton poems and
Beloved, playing Madden with Ray Gunn, shooting midrange
jumpers, listening to Redman, *The Chronic*, and Dionne Far-
ris, and watching the *Eyes on the Prize* episode about Mississippi over and over again on VHS in the library.

I knew enough now about Millsaps to write an essay for my liberal studies course called "Institutional Racism at Millsaps." An editor for the paper heard about the essay from one of my professors and asked if he could run it in the newspaper. He wanted to run it with the subhead "Voice of the Oppressed."

I never used the word "oppressed" and had no idea what an oppressed voice actually sounded like. The editor told me I needed to make the ending of the piece much more colorblind. He said I would lose readers if I kept the focus of the essay on what black students at Millsaps could do to organize, love each other, and navigate institutional racism. He said my primary audience should be white students who wanted to understand what they needed to do about racism on their college campus. After going back and forth, the editor won because it was his newspaper, and I was desperate to be read by white folk.

At least while educating, we must be color-blind, not character blind. This is the only way Millsaps will reach out of the depths of whiteness and better all people equally.

I hated the last paragraph. I hated most of the essay, but I knew Nzola would be impressed that a two-thousand-word essay on institutional racism written by a black boy whose inner thighs she heavy petted almost told these white folk the truth to their faces. I knew Nzola would think almost telling white folk in Mississippi the truth in their paper was as close to winning as black folk could come.

The day after the essay came out, Nzola sent me an e-mail

saying she was proud of me. She asked me what you thought. The essay was the first piece of writing I ever published that I hadn't shown you first.

I'd started using the Internet to send e-mails, but you had not, so I faxed you the piece and called you to ask whether I should accept the opinions editor position I'd been offered for the following year. The editor wanted to call my column "The Key Essay."

Before I could get to the point of the call, you said, "Did they not copyedit your piece, Kiese? I saw four errors on the first page."

"Bye," I said. I didn't have room in my heart or head for your criticism even if you were right.

"Watch your back, Kie. You can't call white folk who think they're liberal or enlightened 'racist' in Mississippi and not expect violent backlash. Reread the books that mean the most to you. Lock your doors. Walk in groups. Strive for perfection. Edit your work. Something feels off. Are you worried about those people shooting you out of the sky?"

"No," I told you. "I'm not even sure what you mean by that."

"Please be careful," you said. "You can always transfer. You said you had to ask me something."

"I'm good. Bye," I said again. "I can't believe you just told me to 'walk in groups.' "

I listened to the Coup and read everything James Baldwin had written that summer. I learned you haven't read anything if you've only read something once or twice. Reading things more than twice was the reader version of revision. I read *The Fire Next Time* over and over again. I wondered how it would read differently had the entire book, and not just the first section, been written to, and for, Baldwin's nephew. I wondered what, and how, Baldwin would have written to his niece. I wondered about the purpose of warning white folk about the coming fire. Mostly, I wondered what black writers weren't writing when we spent so much creative energy begging white folk to change.

Three weeks into the summer, I read an essay from *Nobody Knows My Name* called "Faulkner and Desegregation."

Any real change implies the breakup of the world as one has always known it, the loss of all that gave one an identity, the end of safety.

Baldwin was critiquing Faulkner for holding on to shamefully violent versions of neo-Confederate white Mississippi identity, but I imagined the sentence was written to me. I thought about the safety I found in eating too much, eating too late, eating to run away from memory. I stopped eating red meat, then pork, then chicken, then fish. I stopped eating eggs, then bread, then anything with refined sugar. I started running at night. I added three hundred push-ups a day. Then three hundred sit-ups. I began the summer weighing 309 pounds. In two weeks, I was 289. In a month, I was 279. In two months, I was 255. By the end of the summer, I was 225 pounds.

I jogged three miles before bed, and three miles in the morning. I ate one meal of ramen noodles every other day. When I wasn't reading and running, I wrote a few satirical essays for the paper that caught the attention of students, faculty, and alums of Millsaps. I was the happiest I'd ever been in my life. The day I went under 218 pounds for the first time since seventh grade, Nzola knocked on my door.

"Everyone is talking about your essay," she said.

"Already?"

"Already."

"Everyone who?"

"White folk, chile," she said. "They so mad. But fuck them. You told the truth."

Nzola and I laughed and laughed and laughed until we hugged, turned the lights off, turned the lights on, said we were sorry, and said we were afraid. We laughed as I awkwardly stood up and played Janet Jackson's "Again."

"Weirdo, it's a CD," Nzola said. "You can just put it on repeat."

I messed around with the thing for damn near a minute before Nzola walked over to the stereo and took my hand and my palm against her face. We kissed. We took off almost all our clothes. We started to sweat. I asked Nzola if she minded if I took a shower. She asked if she could come with me. I said yes because I had a new body. We laughed while kissing with the lights on. We laughed while kissing with the lights off. We laughed and loved each other's bodies on a damp yellow frayed towel, on a plastic twin bed, on a floor littered with empty ramen packs, on a yellow brick wall that held up Norman Rockwell's Ruby Bridges painting.

Nzola told me she felt safer when she felt smaller around me, but she said I seemed happier in a smaller body. I asked her how sexy she'd think I was if she could see my cheekbones, my hip bones, my clavicle. I told Nzola losing weight made me feel like I was from the future, like I could literally fly away from folk when I wanted to. Heavy was yesterday.

"You are so crazy," she said.

"I love losing weight," I told her.

145

"Boy, you sound so crazy."

"I'm serious," I said. "My penis shines more since I have less layers, too, right?"

"Kiese Laymon, what are you talking about?"

"I legit feel like my penis is shinier since I lost all that weight. You don't think so? I know y'all don't like a dusty penis."

"I think your penis is shiny enough, Kiese."

"So my penis was dusty when I was heavier, right? Why didn't you tell me to use lotion?"

Nzola laughed and laughed and laughed until she didn't. She grabbed both of my ears and kissed me. "Do you feel home?" she asked me. "Honestly. Next to me?"

"I feel so home," I told her. "Do you?"

"I never want to feel anything else other than what I feel right now for the rest of my life, Kiese. Please stop worrying about the size of your body. And please don't ever stop kissing me."

Two weeks later, Malachi Hunter asked me to come to his office after I got a gun to protect Nzola and me from threatening letters we received. The president of Millsaps, George Harmon, shut down the campus paper and sent a letter to twelve thousand Millsaps alums claiming a satirical essay I wrote for the paper violated the institution's decency guidelines. Half of the letters called me a nigger. Others threatened to take me off that campus if I didn't leave on my own. One, filled with the ashes of all the essays I'd written for the paper, claimed I was going to end up burnt like the ashes if I didn't change and give myself over to God.

I walked from campus to Malachi Hunter's office. After congratulating me on losing so much weight and asking how

to get more definition in his calves, Malachi Hunter asked me, "Who is the richest nigga you know?"

"You are."

"And how much do you think I made last year?"

"A hundred thousand?"

"Nigga, please. I'm rich," he said, and looked at me without blinking like I tried to cut him with a spoon. "Let's say I only made three hundred thousand dollars. Now let's look at your mama's white lawyer friend, Roger."

"Roger who?"

"The white Roger," he said.

"I don't know the white Roger."

"Let's say white Roger made three hundred thousand dollars, too. You following me? My three hundred thousand ain't close to white Roger's three hundred thousand. If I made that little three hundred thousand, I'm still the only nigga with money I know, you see? My girlfriend ain't got no money. The black women I'm trying to fuck, they ain't got no money. My mama and daddy ain't got no money. My sisters and brothers ain't got no money. My uncles ain't got no money. My aunties ain't got no money. The radical organizations I support ain't got no money. The black school I went to ain't got no money. Meanwhile, damn near everyone white around white Roger got at least some land, some inheritance, some kind of money. White Roger might be the poorest person in his family making three hundred thousand."

"I already read *Black Power*," I told him. "I know this."

"You wasting time fighting rich Mississippi white folk for free," he said. "And I'm asking you, right here, for what? You can't fight these folk with no essay. You ain't organized. You ain't got no land. You ain't feeding no one with that shit you

writing. What is it you want white folk to do, and how is whatever they do after reading an essay going to help poor niggas in Mississippi? That's the only question that matters."

"I don't know," I told him.

"I know you don't. You fucking up, Kie," he said. "You fucking up. And we only have a limited number of fuckups before we be fucked up for good. The school has no choice but to get rid of you. You making it so easy for them. Your mama said you getting death threats."

"I am."

"Nobody who wants to kill you is ever going to threaten you. They will kill you, or they won't. There's a difference between deed and word. They will get rid of you, though. It's inevitable. That's already in motion. I don't agree with your mama about much, but we both agree about that."

"Is that all?"

"Just be careful," Malachi Hunter said. "I think you think that school is yours. And Jackson is yours. And Mississippi is yours. Only thing you own is your body. Just be careful."

I wanted to shoot Malachi Hunter in his pinky toe for even mentioning you, but I wanted to shoot him in his ankle for always acting like he knew exactly what black folk should do. Malachi Hunter loved black folk, but even more than black folk, he loved preaching about what black folk were doing wrong. What we were ultimately always doing wrong, according to Malachi Hunter, was not doing what he would do. Even though I wanted to shoot Malachi Hunter, I knew he wasn't all the way wrong about Millsaps or me.

It was too late, though.

Nothing, other than losing weight, felt as good as provoking and really titillating white folk with black words. On the

morning of bid day, Nzola and I were going to our jobs at Ton-o-Fun when we saw drunk members of Kappa Sig and Kappa Alpha fraternities dressed in Afro wigs and Confederate capes. We watched them watch us as we walked to Nzola's car. After one of them said "Write about this," and others started calling me a "nigger" and Nzola a "nigger bitch," I went back to my room to get my gun.

I grabbed a T-ball bat instead, and threw the bat down when we returned to the scene and got closer to the white boys. They surrounded us, and we defended ourselves with words until our words broke. The white boys were blasting Snoop's "Gz and Hustlas" the whole time they were calling us niggers.

When we got to work, we called the local news and told them there was something they might want to see happening on the campus of Millsaps College. We'd only been working at Ton-o-Fun a few weeks and knew if we left we might be fired, but we didn't care. The news crew showed up and got all the footage they needed to paint Millsaps College as the regressive, racist institution I'd been writing about for a semester.

"Come home," you told me on the phone that night. "Do not step foot on that campus again. You've done all you can do. There are some amazing people at that school, but white people's ignorance is not your responsibility. Come home and leave those crazy people alone."

If home wasn't Millsaps, I didn't know where home was. In spite of all the violence and strangeness at school, I felt a kind of freedom and intellectual stimulation at Millsaps that I'd never felt anywhere else in the world. I was targeted, but I felt strangely happy and free.

Nzola and I fought and had sex more frequently since being put on disciplinary probation for defending ourselves against the Kappa Alpha and Kappa Sig fraternities on bid day. The local news stations followed me around campus daily and the NAACP said everything that happened was typical of the bodily terror young endangered black men in this nation face when just trying to get an education.

"All of this is just wrong," Nzola said one night while making a collage on the floor of my room. Her back was against my door. I didn't ask her what she meant, but she kept going. "Those white boys, they called both of us niggers, right? I just wanna make sure I'm not trippin'."

"You ain't trippin'."

"But they called me a nigger and a bitch, right?"

"Right."

"Nigger bitch, right?"

"Right."

"And all these people on the news can talk about is how they were dressed when they said what they said to you?"

"I already—"

"Hold on. A group of big drunk-ass white boys called me a nigger and a bitch. Everyone, including you, heard it. If you know that's what happened, why don't you do something?"

"I tried to fight them that day. I tried to fight them the next day. If I do anything else, they'll kick me out."

"I'm asking why you didn't say that they called me a nigger and a bitch when they put those fucking microphones in your face."

"Every time I did an interview, I talked about you and why we did what we did," I told her. "Didn't I do that? You want these news folk to be talking more about you?"

"I'm not saying that," she said. "I'm saying people are acting like you were out there fighting back by yourself. And
you weren't. I'm saying if I wrote the same essays you wrote,
no one would care. You take all these damn women's studies courses and you haven't said one fucking word about no
'patriarchy' or 'sexism' or 'intersectionality' these past two
weeks."

"Wait, wait, wait. How do you know nothing would happen if you wrote the same shit I wrote?"

"I know."

"How do you know?"

"I know."

I sucked on my teeth. "Right, but how do you know? You
making excuses," I said, looking at Nzola, who was biting the
inside of her bottom lip.

"Excuses for what?"

"You a funny woman."

"You a funny nigga," she said. "Excuses for what, Kiese?"

"When I was staying up forty-eight hours straight, writing
all this shit, you could've been making art, too, but you were
on the phone playing doctor with that Trapper James, MD–ass
nigga up in DC," I told her. "You'd still be playing doctor if the
nigga hadn't decided to start playing with another girl. Now
you wanna say the only reason my art landed was because I'm
a black boy and you a black girl? Sometimes I wonder if I'm
talking to you or your stepmama. You a funny-ass woman.
Believe that."

Nzola stood up, dusted off the back of her khakis, and
applied a taste of ChapStick. I knew what was coming. I
wanted it to come. Nzola cocked her arm back and jabbed
me in the left eye.

She sat back down and kept working on her collage.

This wasn't the first, second, third, or fourth time I let her punch me in my face. Almost every time she did it, I'd said something about her stepmother. I knew it was coming. I hoped it would come. I thought I deserved it.

It always made me feel lighter.

We had sex because that's how we apologized. Nzola talked about how we might be more useful organizing with other black students in Jackson, Malachi Hunter, and you to fight the Ayers case. Y'all had been fighting to stop the state from closing or merging historically black colleges and universities in Mississippi, including Jackson State. I told her she was right but I had no intention of stopping the work I was doing on the Millsaps campus. When we woke up, Nzola said I still didn't understand. I told her I did. I told Nzola *she* didn't understand.

She said she had to.

Nzola said there was no way two drunk fraternities of black men with their shirts off could threaten a white girl going to work, call the white girl a "cracker bitch," and then have that white girl be found guilty of anything. "How do you not see it?" she kept saying.

"I see it," I told her. "I so see it. For real. But what you want me to do?"

Nzola and I were in the middle of our city, lying wet, resentful, and nearly naked on top of a plastic twin mattress separating our backs from a loaded pistol. We hated where we were. We hated ourselves. We hated fighting, fucking, fighting, fucking, fighting over who was most violated by a spiteful college president, confused white classmates, and the gated institution we took out thousands of dollars in loans to attend.

"What are you thinking?" Nzola asked the back of my head.

"I'm thinking something bad is about to happen. What about you?"

"I'm knowing a lot of bad things already did."

SOON

President George Harmon told you I was lucky not to be thrown in jail for taking *The Red Badge of Courage* from the library without checking it out. He claimed if Millsaps turned the security tape of my taking the library book over to the police, they'd arrest me on sight. In addition to kicking me out of college and forbidding me from trespassing on Millsaps property, Harmon gave my work to a local psychologist who claimed I needed immediate help interacting with white folk before they would even consider reenrolling me.

I smiled while sitting across from you and George Harmon that day, not because I was happy but because I really didn't think any student in the country could be kicked out of school for taking *The Red Badge of Courage* out of the library. I didn't think it was possible because I didn't think my teachers in the middle of my city would let it happen. I assumed when we walked out of that office, all my professors would be waiting to meet with Harmon. I knew Jackson State would never kick one of your students out for improperly taking a library book and returning it because they'd have to deal with you and your colleagues if they did. In the few minutes between when Harmon gave you the letter outlining my discipline and our walk out to the car, I realized that my professors at Millsaps were nothing like you.

By the time you put the key in the ignition of the Oldsmobile, we both accepted I did not make it. I was no longer a student. I allowed Millsaps College to shoot me out of the sky, and any school I thought of transferring to would see I was put on disciplinary probation for fighting and kicked out of college for theft. For the second time in my life since that night when Malachi Hunter spent the night after punching you in your eye, I felt waves of shame that made me not want to be alive.

Ray Gunn introduced me to the word "antiblack" two weeks before I got kicked out of school. I was talking to him about patriarchy and he nodded and said patriarchy was like antiblackness. He said the problem with fighting white folk was even the most committed of black folk had to deal with their own relationships to "antiblackness." I told him how LaThon and I used to say and believe black abundance. He said I should have learned a lot more about black abundance before I got kicked out of school for making educating white folks at Millsaps my homework.

He was right. Nzola begged me to do more organizing with folk at Jackson State. Malachi Hunter begged me not to waste time fighting white Mississippians for free. Ray Gunn told me Millsaps would do anything to get rid of ungrateful black students. Grandmama told me to put my head down and get good at the parts of school I disliked. Dr. Jerry Ward, who was still teaching at Tougaloo College and wrote the introduction to the version of *Black Boy* we read in class, suggested I transfer to Oberlin and work with Calvin Hernton long before I got kicked out of school. You begged me not to let those folk shoot me out the sky. I'm sorry for not listening to you. I didn't listen to one black person who loved me because listening to black folk who loved me brought me little pleasure. I'd fallen in love with provoking white folk, which really meant I'd fallen in love with begging white folk to free us by demanding that they radically love themselves more.

I enrolled at Jackson State and spent most of my nights at Ray Gunn's house listening to him theorize about everything from why white dudes whose noses were too close to their top lips were always assholes to how there was no way a black president could actually make life better for poor black people, but when he started taking care of his little sister from Chicago, I was forced to stay home with you. Going to classes every day at a school where I was conceived, born, and raised, a place filled with dynamic black students and tired, dynamic black professors, was everything I thought it would be. But going to school every day where you worked was everything I feared. My teachers told you how I performed in class, whether I came to class, approximately how late I was. The worst part was that every day I left Jackson State, I found my way back to the campus of Millsaps to see Gunn and Nzola. And nearly every time I showed up, security showed up and made me leave.

One Friday morning, a day after you pulled a gun on me for talking back to you about whether the transfer application to Oberlin should be typed or handwritten, I sat naked in a cold tub of water with your .22 cocked, tapping my temple. We'd been told by three schools that they couldn't even consider my transfer application because I'd been kicked out of Millsaps for fighting and stealing.

I didn't know how to pray anymore, but I knew how to listen. I got on my knees in that bathtub listening for deliverance, forgiveness, and redemption. I didn't hear any of that. I heard the words "be" and "meager" and "murmur" and "nan" and "gumption" in Grandmama's voice. All those words sounded like love to me. I didn't know what was wrong with me. But I knew I never wanted you or Grandmama to live in a world that sounded like the world might sound if I shot a bullet through my skull in your bathtub.

Despite pleas from you and Nzola, I started working at Grace House, a home that offered care for homeless HIV-positive men in Jackson. Grace House was a huge two-story home shielded by a massive gray wooden gate. It was thirty yards from Millsaps, literally on a street called Millsaps Avenue, in the North End. The first day I stepped through the gate, I wondered why the house was located in the poorest, blackest neighborhood in Jackson, and why a house for homeless HIV-positive men in Jackson could never be in a white wealthy neighborhood.

Most of the men at Grace House were black. Some saw the stories on the news about my suspension from Millsaps. They joked about how I was going to steal all the chewy Chips Ahoy! out the kitchen the first week I worked there. I never knew where to throw my eyes when they told me day after day how God had a plan for me, and I'd soon understand that plan. The brothers were free to come and go at Grace House, but most of them talked like brothers I'd met just recently released from the penitentiary. I appreciated what they said, but the goofy eighth grader in me appreciated how sincere they were with every word. They were quick to explain how getting kicked out of college for stealing and returning a library book was nothing more than a complicated annoyance.

It's too simple to say the brothers at Grace House gave me perspective. I'm not sure they gave me anything, other than some of the funniest stories I'd ever heard and access to the painful changes in their bodies. Those stories gave me time and space to shrink back into my comfortable position as a listener. They reminded me I'd been living in a pulpy fiction the past year at Millsaps. They reminded me directly and indirectly I was not the center of the world. I was not nearly as heavy as I thought. There was actually nothing big or heavy about me when I walked into Grace House every day. I was the care provider who liked to read Toni Morrison, watch basketball, watch *Martin*, and do push-ups, not the care provider who liked to read comic books, do crossword puzzles, and watch *Seinfeld*, which really meant that to them I was that other paid listener who they trusted to never reveal their names or identities to anyone outside of Grace House.

I listened to the pauses, repetitions, and holes in their stories as much as I listened to the aches and changes of all their bodies. All the brothers I cared for at Grace House told stories about cars, sports, clothes, politics, food, and families but never talked about how they contracted HIV or whom they might have infected. Their stories were as differently shaped as they were, but they all agreed contracting HIV saved their lives. The first few times I heard this, I nodded and even said "I hear that," but I never fully understood how something so seemingly full of death could actually save a life.

Outside of Grace House, Nzola wouldn't kiss me anymore. She claimed I worked at Grace House because I was HIV-positive and I wanted to be around my people. I'd only had sexual relationships with two women in my life. Neither of those women told me they were HIV-positive and whenever Gunn and I gave blood or plasma for money, we knew they were checking our blood for the virus. I got tested again anyway just to prove to Nzola I was working at Grace House because I wanted to, not because I wanted to "be around my people."

When the test came back negative, I told Nzola the results, knowing she'd have to say she didn't believe me. We'd gone from smiling over greasy pieces of Red Velvet cake to sucking teeth and not even looking at each other over the results of an HIV test.

Every time I saw Nzola after the results came back, we barely spoke other than her asking, "What are you going to do with yourself? Why are you just giving up?"

When I told Nzola on a ride home that Oberlin College might accept my transfer application because of what happened at Millsaps, not in spite of what happened at Millsaps, she cried in front of me for the first time in thirteen months. "I feel like you're trying to leave me in this shit by my fucking self."

I reminded Nzola they'd only accepted my transfer application. When Nzola dropped me off at your house, we hugged. "You feel so small," she said. "I don't know what's wrong with us. Is there anything you want to say?"

Nzola walked with me to the mailbox. On top of all the bills you left in the box, there was a thin piece of mail from Oberlin College. I knew it was my rejection letter. "I don't think so," I said.

"Take care, Kiese," Nzola said as she walked back to her car. "Please eat. I worry one day your mama is gonna call me and say you just disappeared."

It was too late for that. We'd fought, lost, fought again, and both disappeared already. "That won't happen," I told

Nzola as she reversed out of your yard. "I'm sorry about all of this."

That night, I stretched out in the driveway and looked at the stars. For the first time in years, I thought about waiting for you to come home the day I ran away from Beulah Beauford's house. Back then I wanted all my seasons to be Mississippi seasons, no matter how strange, hot, or terrifying. Now I felt something else. I didn't want to float in, under, and around all the orange-red stars in our galaxy if our galaxy was Mississippi. I wanted to look at Mississippi from other stars and I didn't ever want to come home again.

Three months later, you walked me out of the house into the passenger seat of your Oldsmobile with tears in your eyes. Ray was in the driver's seat. He was going to drive me up to Oberlin, and you were going to drive his Impala while he was gone. You and I spent those three months tolerating each other, and really preparing for this day. The shade of the pine trees made both of us colder than we should have been.

"I just love you, Kie," you said. "I'm so scared."

"Scared of what?"

"You've never left me before. I've never been down here, in all this, without you. I just feel like my child, my best friend is leaving me." You wrapped your arms around my chest and I kissed the top of your braids. "How did you get so small? It wasn't supposed to be like this. Maybe I can visit Oberlin for Thanksgiving."

"Oberlin has a fall break in October."

"Just come back soon, Kie," you said. "Do you promise?"

"I will," I told you. "For real. I'll be back in October. I promise. I will be back so soon."

160

I will not be back soon.

I will attend Oberlin College. I will get caught stealing a frame for your birthday from the college bookstore. I will learn under Calvin Hernton how to be the black southern writer Margaret Walker wanted me to be. I will read *The Cancer Journals*. I will learn to get good at the things I didn't want to get good at. I will listen to Christopher Wallace and Tupac Shakur die. I will see creases, hear whiffs, and feel futurist pinches in the work of Octavia Butler and Outkast. I will practice. I will write about the holes in the ground in the woods across the street from Grandmama's house.

I will not be back soon.

I will feel like a good dude for not "technically" having sex with anyone but my girlfriend. I will feel like a good dude. I will call myself a feminist. I will fall in love with friends who fall in love with me. I will listen to friends talk about their experiences with sex and violence and confusion. I will gently ask questions. I will not tell those friends what my body remembered in our bedroom and the bedrooms of Beulah Beauford's house in Mississippi.

I will not be back soon.

I will forget how the insides of my thighs feel when rubbed raw. I will play on the basketball team. I will think 190 pounds is too heavy so I will jog three miles before every practice and game. I will sit in saunas for hours draped in thermals, sweatpants, and sweatshirts. I will make a family of people who cannot believe I was ever heavy. I will become a handsome, fine, together brother with lots of secrets. I will realize there is no limit to the amount of harm handsome, fine, together brothers with lots of secrets can do. I will learn to love and artfully use the Internet on A-level of the library.

I will get a Mellon undergraduate fellowship. I will apply to get an MFA and PhD at Indiana University because the poet Yusef Komunyakaa teaches there. I will walk across the stage at Oberlin College graduation, where I will hug you and my father.

I will not be back soon.

I will never forget the day I told you I'd be back soon, the day I burst your heart wide open, the day I left Mississippi, the day you called me your child, your best friend, your reason for living. I will write about home. I will do everything I can to never feel what I felt those last few years in Mississippi. I will bend. I will break. I will build. I will recover.

I will not be back soon.

Ray Gunn hugged you and promised we'd drive your car carefully. We backed out of the driveway. You walked into the street sobbing into your hands. I should have been crying because you were crying. I tried. I learned how to lie from you but I never learned how to make myself cry. I told Ray to reverse the car. He put it in reverse and I jumped out and hugged your neck.

"Come back, Kie," you said. "Please."

"I'll be back soon," I whispered in your ear, and jumped back in the car. "I'll be back soon," I yelled out the window as we shrunk out of each other's sight. This felt different. "I'll be back soon. Don't worry. I love you. I promise. I will be back home so soon."

IV.

ADDICT AMERICANS.

GREENS

You were in Grandmama's living room delicately placing a blinking black angel with a fluorescent mink coat on top of her Christmas tree while Uncle Jimmy and I were examining each other's bodies in a one-bedroom apartment in Bloomington, Indiana. I was in my final year of graduate school. Uncle Jimmy and I were having a contest to see who could make their forearms veinier. "Shit, sport," Uncle Jimmy said as he hugged me. "You eating a lot of spinach in grad school or what? You look like you training for the league."

I was twenty-six years old, 183 pounds. My body fat was 8 percent.

Uncle Jimmy was six-three and so skinny that his eyes, which were nearly always yolk yellow, looked like they wanted to pop out of his head. He wore the same Chicago Bears sweatshirt, same gray church slacks, same church shoes he wore when he was forty pounds heavier.

When I asked him if anything was wrong, Uncle Jimmy said, "This blood pressure medicine the doctor got me on, it make it hard for a nigga to keep weight on. That's all. Is it okay for me to say 'nigga' around you now? I know you're a professor like your mama and shit now."

I told Uncle Jimmy I was a graduate instructor and a graduate student. "That's a long way from a professor. I think I wanna teach high school. But regardless, you can always say 'nigga' and any other word you want around me. I'm not my mama."

On the way to Mississippi, we stopped at gas station after gas station. Uncle Jimmy went to the bathroom for ten minutes each time. I cranked up *Aquemini* and did push-ups and jumping jacks outside the van while he did whatever he needed to do. He eventually came back with pints of butter pecan ice cream and big bags of Lay's Salt & Vinegar.

"Want some, nephew?" he asked.

"Naw," I said over and over again. "I'm good."

"You good?"

"I'm good," I told him. I didn't tell him I was running eleven miles, playing two hours of ball, and eating eight hundred calories a day. I didn't tell him I gleefully passed out the previous week in the checkout line at Kroger. I didn't tell him a cashier named Laurie asked if I was "diabetic or a dope fiend" when I woke up. I didn't tell him the skinnier my body got, the more it knew what was going to happen, just as much as it remembered where it had been.

Uncle Jimmy looked at me, with Lay's Salt & Vinegar grease all over his mouth, like my nose was a fitted hat. "Let me find out you went from fucking a white girl to eating like a white girl."

"I just love losing weight," I told him. "That's really all it is. I just love losing weight."

"You just love losing weight?" Uncle Jimmy was dying laughing. "My nephew went to grad school and now he turning into a white girl. You just love losing weight? That's damn near the craziest shit I heard in thirty years, Kie. Who say shit like that? You just love losing weight?"

Somewhere around Little Rock, Arkansas, we stopped at a

truck stop. Uncle Jimmy started telling me a story about one of his friends he worked with at the Caterpillar plant. He said he and this friend served the same tour in Vietnam and had been to Alcoholics Anonymous three times each.

"So yeah, he always talking big about all the Martell he drank over the weekend and all the pussy he be getting," Uncle Jimmy said. "Always talking about how the white man'll do anything to keep a nigga down. And he start talking about spoiled-ass Bush. I told him we been known there ain't nothing the white man won't do. He said he agreed. But soon as the white boss man come around, this nigga tuck his head into his shoulders like a gotdamn turtle. Steady grinning and jiving them white folk to death."

I asked Uncle Jimmy why his friend acted one way around him and another way around the white boss man. "Shit," he said, nervously tapping his foot under the table, "you know how some niggas are, addicted to giving the white man whatever he want whenever he want it. Not me, though. You know that."

Uncle Jimmy was right. I'd spent the last four years of my life reading and creating art invested in who we were, what we knew, how we remembered, and what we imagined when white folk weren't around. For me, that vision had everything to do with Grandmama's porch. Every time I sat down to write, I imagined sitting on that porch with layers of black Mississippi in front of and behind me.

While Uncle Jimmy was in the bathroom, I called Grandmama on the pay phone to let her know we were going to be home later than we expected.

You picked up.

"Hey," I said. "What y'all doing?"

"Hey, Kie, we're on our way to the hospital. Tell Jimmy to meet us there. Is he drunk?"

"Naw," I said. "He's not drunk. He's in the bathroom right now. Is Grandmama okay?"

You told me Grandmama had fallen asleep in her chair after complaining of dizziness. When you went to take her wig off, you saw blood on the inside of the wig. You told me you looked at the back of Grandmama's head and saw this infected hole oozing with puss. "Please don't tell Jimmy," you said. "If he gets even a little stressed, he'll start drinking like a dolphin."

"I don't think dolphins drink, though."

"Just bring your ass directly to the hospital, Kie."

When Uncle Jimmy finally made it back to the car, he was flying on something more than Hennessy or weed. He handed me a Black Ice air freshener he bought and told me to make the world smell this good. When I asked him what he meant, he said, "Drive this van, nephew. Drive this shit. Make the world smell this good." Uncle Jimmy could barely open his eyes or close his mouth. "Don't use the brakes like you did last time, nephew. Drive this shit all the way home."

I'd heard Grandmama whimper over the loss of her best friend and her sisters. I'd heard Grandmama yell at Uncle Jimmy for daring to disrespect her in her house. I'd never heard Grandmama scream while begging the Lord to have mercy on her until that night in the hospital.

Uncle Jimmy wasn't as high anymore. He and HaLester Myers, Grandmama's new husband, were sitting in the waiting room, avoiding each other's eyes, watching news about Bush and the Supreme Court. You, Aunt Linda, and Aunt

Sue were down the hall talking shit about Uncle Jimmy. You blamed whatever he was going through on what he saw and did in Vietnam. Aunt Linda blamed alcohol. Aunt Sue blamed all of us for not praying for him more.

I walked away from y'all and went to Grandmama's room.

With one hand in the pockets of my mesh shorts, and one hand holding hers, I told Grandmama it was going to be okay. Grandmama said she had faith in the white doctor who was taking care of her. She kept calling him "the white-man doctor," though he was really a short, light-complexioned black man with a dry, red Afro.

"The white-man doctor got my best interest at heart," she said. "Grandmama will be fine directly."

The black doctor with the dry red Afro asked me to leave the room because they had to do a small procedure. He said the infection was deeper than he thought. It started in the middle of her head and went down the back of her neck. "We're gonna help her with this pain," he told me. "The infection is seeping into her bloodstream."

I walked out of the room but he didn't close the door behind me. "Lord Jesus," Grandmama kept saying before she screamed. "Please have mercy. Please have mercy." I knew, but didn't want to admit, why Grandmama was screaming, why the black doctor with the dry red Afro didn't give her enough anesthetic, why he thought cutting a full inch and a half deep into the back of her scalp was for her own good.

Folk always assumed black women would recover but never really cared if black women recovered. I knew Grandmama would act like she recovered before thanking Jesus for keeping her alive. She would never publicly reckon with damage done to her insides and outsides at the hands of people who claimed to have her best interest at heart. She would just thank Jesus for getting through the other side of suffering. Thanking Jesus for getting us through situations we should have never been in was one of our family's superpowers.

I spent the night in the room sitting in a chair next to Grandmama's bed and holding her hand. Grandmama didn't say a word. She just looked out the window of the room, with her cheek pressed into the thin mattress until the sun came up.

The next morning, after I went for an early morning jog, Uncle Jimmy walked into Grandmama's room. "These folk got me looking like a mummy, Jimmy Earl," Grandmama said, before hugging Uncle Jimmy's neck and talking about how skinny we'd both gotten since the last time she'd seen us. I told her she needed to do a better job of taking care of herself.

"You need to mind your business, Kie," she said, "and don't lose no more weight or your head liable to bop on down the road."

"How can a head bop down a road, Grandmama?"

"You know what I mean, Kie," she said, laughing at herself before directing her attention to Uncle Jimmy. "Why you ain't eating, Jimmy Earl? You hear me?"

Grandmama looked at Uncle Jimmy and me standing side by side. She kept blinking her eyes in slow motion. The slow blinking was even worse than the eye twitching. Everyone in the family knew the slow blinking meant Grandmama was double disgusted with whatever she was looking at.

"I'm eating, Mama," Uncle Jimmy said all of a sudden.

"What you eating, Jimmy Earl?"

Uncle Jimmy looked at me. "Gizzards," he said. "Lots of spinach, too. All the spinach and gizzards I can eat."

"Boy, you ain't seen a leaf of no spinach. Why you ain't eating, Jimmy Earl? Don't get to lying off in this hospital."

"I ate spinach the whole trip down," Uncle Jimmy told Grandmama, while looking at me. "The whole trip down. Didn't I eat spinach, Kie?"

Grandmama's slow-blinking eyes dared me to lie so I kept my mouth shut and nodded up and down until I said, "Grandmama, what you think of Bush and them stealing that election?"

"Ain't nothing the white man is too shamed to do, except do right by us. And it's always some ol' big-head black man who should know better trying to help the white man harm us."

"Talking about Clarence Thomas?"

"Yeah, that ol' big-head man know good and well these folk been stealing everything from us that ain't nailed down since before I was born. I knew that man wasn't right from when he sat on TV talking about a high-tech lynching when he got caught harassing that black woman. What her name is, Kie?"

"Anita Hill."

"Right. Right. Anita Hill. All the education you got and you surprised they stole that election?" Grandmama asked me. "All that schooling, and you didn't know what they was planning with all that gerrymandering? Kie, did Jimmy Earl eat spinach when y'all drove up here?"

I got up, stretched my calves, and weighed myself on the scale beside Grandmama's bed. "I slept most of the way down here, but maybe," I told her, and walked out of the room so Uncle Jimmy could tell all the lies he wanted to with no shame.

171

Stepping on the scale in Grandmama's hospital room was the first time I'd stepped on a scale since leaving Indiana. The scale on the bottom floor of the gym at Indiana was the sleekest, sturdiest, most precise scale I'd ever stepped on. If I weighed myself, then took just a half sip of water or spit a few times, I could see a change in my weight. I weighed myself in the bottom of that gym before and after every workout, before and after every meal. I also got a tape measure to measure my waist every morning when I woke up. I came to Indiana with a thirty-three-inch waist and I managed to get it down to twenty-eight inches in two and a half years. Twenty-eight inches was good, and it was so far from forty-eight inches at my heaviest, but I knew I could get my waist even smaller if I worked harder.

Grandmama was released from the hospital three days later. When I got to her house late Saturday night, Grandmama, Aunt Sue, Aunt Linda, and you were sitting around the TV watching *The Color Purple* in silence. Every time y'all watched it, it seemed like the first time. Y'all didn't cry. Y'all didn't move. Y'all just breathed deeply and made sure part of your body was touching the body of the woman next to you.

After the movie, while everyone in the living room was talking about how no good Clarence Thomas was for helping George Bush steal the election, you asked Aunt Linda and me if we wanted to go to the casino in Philadelphia. Aunt Linda, who lived in Vegas, swore that the Mississippi casinos were too country to hit, but she loved how reverential folk in those country casinos were to her.

"Vegas, honey," she loved to say when folk asked about her elaborate wigs and her two-inch fingernails layered in ruby-red nail polish and studded diamonds. "I'm from Vegas, honey."

I went in the bathroom to weigh myself before getting in the car, but Grandmama's scale was gone.

Aunt Linda talked from Forest to Philadelphia about this video poker game and what she'd have to hit to get off the machine. When Aunt Linda asked you how much you'd have to hit, you didn't answer her question.

The Golden Moon Casino in Philadelphia, Mississippi, was a windowless space of smoke, free alcohol, emergency lights, and ding-ding-dings. You didn't have to play to hear the ding-ding-dings and see the emergency lights. I didn't understand why anyone would put a dollar in a machine you'd probably lose when you could just watch folk, drink all you wanted, and listen to ding-ding-dings all night for free.

I sat in front of the machine across the casino floor from you, sipping diet pop, watching you spend every dollar you had in your pocket. I watched you rummage through your purse for enough quarters, dimes, nickels, and pennies to take to the casino cage and get a few dollar bills. I watched you take those dollar bills and slide the money in the machine you were sitting at a few minutes earlier.

When you saw me watching you, I walked over and gave you the forty dollars Grandmama had given me for Christmas and the sixty dollars I had in my wallet. I watched you slide the five twenties in the same machine. In less than a minute, you walked over to Aunt Linda and sat next to her as she played. Neither one of you said a word. Aunt Linda eventually gave you what looked like another twenty and turned her back to you.

You went back to the same machine. When money was

gone, you looked over both shoulders and watched me watch you again. You walked over to me and asked if I brought my credit card. I told you I hadn't had a credit card since somebody stole mine at Millsaps a few years ago.

"You need a credit card, Kie," you said. "That's how you build up your credit."

I wanted to say so much, but we'd made it through Christmas without fighting and I didn't know what I would do or feel if you slapped the taste out of my mouth after I'd given you my last money at a casino.

When we got home, you walked in Grandmama's room, spread out across the foot of the bed, and told me to close the bedroom door.

"I don't feel good, Ma," you said to Grandmama.

"What you reckon it is?" Grandmama asked.

"Kie," you said, "close the damn door."

"Okay," I said. "But why?"

"Because I said so, Kie. Just close the damn door."

Before I left for Indiana the next morning, Grandmama asked if I would go outside on the porch. Everyone else was either watching Tiger Woods beat white men in golf or they were in the kitchen assembling two-pound plates of food and slicing up German chocolate cake and sweet potato pie to take home. I sat in the same yellow peeling chair I sat in fifteen years earlier. I told Grandmama I couldn't believe how full and green the woods looked when I was a kid. She told me no part of the world stops changing just because you leave it. "Why you tapping your foot like Jimmy Earl, Kie?"

I didn't even notice I was tapping my toes on the porch.

"I don't know," I told her. "I probably need to go for a run. I want you to take better care of yourself, Grandmama. For real. Don't wait until the last minute if something is wrong with your body. And don't try to fix your body if you know someone else can fix it better. You getting enough exercise?"

"You gone exercise crazy," Grandmama said. "You lost all that little fat and now you trying to coach folk? The worst kinds of teachers be the teachers that teach other folk how to be like them. We all got ears. We all know when folk talking down to us. My whole life, I been exercising. You seen them big ol' bags of cans in the backyard? I walk up and down this twice a day picking up cans to take to the can man. Them nice Mexican folk off in the trailer park next door, they brang me some of they cans after seeing me walk up and down this road. So I get my exercise. Worry about yourself." I laughed off Grandmama's comment. "Listen, Kie. Something in the milk ain't clean. I want you to call your mama and Jimmy Earl more."

"I talk to Mama every few days, Grandmama."

"Well, talk every day then," she said. "Twice a day. Call your uncle Jimmy Earl more, too." I looked at Grandmama, who was now playing with the bandages wrapped around her head. "Do you hear me? It ain't but about one or maybe two ways to get a blessing. But it's a million ways to give a blessing away. And some folk, they be so good at giving away blessings. You give away your blessings enough, one day the Lord will up and take whatever blessing you need and leave you with nan blessing at all."

"Nan blessing, Grandmama?" I asked, bent over laughing. "You need your own show."

"Nan blessing, Kie. I'm telling you what I know. And I

ain't just talking about no money. I'm talking about anything the Lord seen fit to bless you with."

"I hear you, Grandmama," I said. "Can I ask you something?"

"What is it, Kie? I'm not trying to talk about nothing crazy out here on this porch now."

"I hear everything you're saying about blessings and talking to Mama. I'm just wondering what happened to your scale?"

"Lord have mercy," Grandmama said, and started slow-blinking her eyes. "Sometimes I wonder if your bread is all the way done."

"My bread is so done, Grandmama," I told her. "I just really love losing weight."

Grandmama's eyes slowly and steadily blinked out on that porch that day.

On our way up to Indiana, I did not eat or drink. I had no way of knowing how much I weighed until I paid the dollar to weigh myself on the raggedy bathroom scale at a rest stop in Tennessee. According to the scale, I was 186 pounds, up two pounds from when I weighed myself at the hospital.

When we crossed the Arkansas state line, Uncle Jimmy stopped at a KFC and ordered some gizzards to go. A few miles down the road, we stopped at a grocery store that sold hot food. Uncle Jimmy told me to wait in the van. He came out with nothing and headed to another grocery store that served hot food. This time, he came out with two beige Styrofoam containers filled with greens and corn bread. He was trying to right his wrong.

"Want some, nephew?"

"Naw," I told him. "I'm good."

Uncle Jimmy sat in the parking lot of that grocery store eating what must have been a pound of greens and corn bread. When he was done with both containers, he told me Grandmama complained to the rest of the family that I'd been in school long enough. According to Uncle Jimmy, Grandmama said it was time for me to get a real job so I could help the family with money. Uncle Jimmy lied a lot, but I knew it was Grandmama's style to tell the truth about whoever wasn't in the room.

I told Uncle Jimmy I made about twelve thousand dollars a year at Indiana. After paying my rent and my bills, I had about two hundred and twenty dollars left every month. A hundred went to the student loans from Millsaps I defaulted on when you left all the notices in the mailbox. Forty went to Grandmama. Twenty went to savings. Sixty went to food.

"Mama said she want you to get a real job," he said again. "So you should go ahead and get on that directly. Make some real money."

I decided in Uncle Jimmy's van that instead of working toward my PhD, I'd take my MFA and apply for a fellowship that placed grad students of color in liberal arts colleges to teach for two years. If I could get the fellowship, I'd revise the books I was working on while teaching, then I'd try to sell them and get a decent paying job somewhere else.

When Uncle Jimmy dropped me off, he didn't hug my neck. He didn't dap me up. He thanked me for not telling on him and told me he'd see me next year.

"Sometimes I wonder if maybe we could talk on the phone?" I asked him from outside the van.

Uncle Jimmy took off without responding to my question. I didn't know exactly what Uncle Jimmy was putting in his body during our trip down to Mississippi. I knew on our trip back up to Indiana he'd eaten more greens than I'd ever seen a human eat in one sitting. After he dropped me off, I knew he was going to get back to flying and crashing because flying and crashing were what people in our family did when we were alone, ashamed, and scared to death.

After jogging up the stairs to my apartment, I got on my knees and thanked God I wasn't flying and crashing like Uncle Jimmy, or crying and scratching crusted scabs out of my head like Grandmama, or moping and regretting all the money I lost in a casino like you. I rubbed my palms up and down my abs, searching for new muscles. I ran my fingers over my pecs, flexed both to see which one was more defined. I slid my hands into the gap between my hard thighs and squeezed as hard as I could. I traced the veins in my calves down to my ankles and back up behind my knees. Whenever I looked at myself in the mirror, I still saw a 319-pound fat black boy from Jackson. When I touched myself or saw how much I weighed or my percentage of body fat, I knew I'd created a body. I knew I'd made a body disappear.

I got off my knees and asked God to help y'all confront the memories you were running from. I asked God to help all of y'all lose your weight. I planned to do everything I could not to give my blessings away and provide for y'all. The first thing I had to do was sprint down to the gym before it closed. I wanted to know exactly how much I weighed so I could decide if it was okay for me to eat or drink before going to bed.

TERRORS

You were parked at an auto shop in Brandon, Mississippi, hoping a mechanic would fix your Subaru on credit while I was sleeping on the floor of my new office in Poughkeepsie, New York. I was a 180-pound black adjunct professor at Vassar College. I had 6 percent body fat and a few hundred dollars to my name.

When I told you where I slept, you said in order to embody black excellence, especially at a place white northerners deemed elite, I must maintain healthy distance from my colleagues and never let them see me "disheveled." I heard, that first week, from more white colleagues than I could count how lucky I was to be at Vassar. When you were my age, you'd been teaching at Jackson State for two years. I was six years old. I wondered if your black colleagues, who were your professors a few years earlier, called you lucky to be back teaching at Jackson State.

I remember watching you give everything you had to your students those first few years we were back in Mississippi. Nearly all of your first students were black, first-generation students from Mississippi. You spent sixteen-hour days meeting students on weekends, talking to worried parents on the phone, helping students with their financial aid forms, finding food for them when we didn't even have enough money for food ourselves. We talked more when I got to Vassar than

179

we'd talked since I was twelve years old. I lied a lot and kept the personal surrounding my professional life a secret, but you loved when I asked you questions about how to navigate my life as a young black professor.

"The world was out to smother me and my kids," you told me a week after I arrived at Vassar. "My job as a teacher was to help them breathe with excellence and discipline in the classroom. The ones that love you, they become what you model. Don't forget that. Help them breathe by modeling responsible love in the classroom every single day. The most important thing a teacher can do is give their students permission to be loving and excellent."

I realized that first week of teaching I had far more in common with my students than my colleagues, most of whom were white and older than Grandmama. Even though I was the youngest professor at the college, I dressed that first day like the excellent, disciplined, elegant black man you wanted me to be. I rocked a baggy brown wool suit and shiny Stacy Adams loafers. The suit was way baggier than when you gave it to me for graduation from Oberlin. By the end of the first week of classes, the suit was gone. If I wore a blazer, I wore it on top of a T-shirt and jeans. Being comfortable around my students made too much sense.

My first week of class, I understood that none of my students, especially the black and brown ones who gravitated to me, wanted to be treated as noble exceptions to their communities. They wanted to be loved, inspired, protected, and heard. They didn't want to be punished or unfairly disciplined for navigating the craziness that came with leaving home to sleep, eat, and drink with people they didn't know while learning in haunted classrooms and dorms. Like nearly every black professor I knew from the Deep South, I expected to protect my students from security, police, and malicious administrations. I expected to pick them up from police stations, train stations, and emergency rooms. I didn't expect to fail them as much as I did. I misgendered my students when they asked if I could help push the college to cover the cost of transitioning because they'd been disowned by their parents for being transgender. I made my students engage with art that attacked them for being queer, femme, black, and poor. I came into my James Baldwin lecture after the Virginia Tech shootings and told the one Asian American boy in the class, who happened to be Vietnamese, I was free if he ever wanted to talk about violence. I asked one of my Chicana students who told me her family had been deported if she knew when they'd be back, and if she wanted to publish an essay about it.

I found more ways to fail and harm my kids than I ever imagined. Every time I failed them, I knew I thought I was doing something you would never have done.

When I told you about security coming in my office, asking to see my ID when pictures of you and me sat on my desk, you said, "Terror looks like this." I laughed off your comment and told you how happy I was to have access to a copier, printing paper, one of the most beautiful libraries on earth, unlimited smoothies, a meditation spot called Shakespeare garden, and a make-out spot called Sunset Lake. I knew the job would be challenging, but I was essentially getting paid to teach, serve, and write for seven months of the year. I tried to convince you that my relationship with students at Vassar was home, and the two rooms of that home were our classrooms and my office. You told me to learn from your mistakes and understand that pain awaited any worker in this country who made a home of their job.

I should have listened to you.

On September 11, 2001, a week and a half after school started, I learned I was as far from home as I could be and still be within the United States. On September 12, I watched my Pakistani neighbors plaster their Corollas with I LOVE THE U.S.A. bumper stickers and dress their newborn in a red, white, and blue outfit I'd seen at Marshalls.

I didn't understand.

Three days later, on September 15, I decided to take the Metro North down to New York City to volunteer at Ground Zero. The Poughkeepsie station was packed with slack-faced soldiers holding M-16s next to ignorant-looking German shepherds. When I got on the train, a dark-skinned South Asian family was seated in front of me. The entire family wore clothing in variations of red, white, and blue. The father placed a suitcase above their seat; on it a sticker proclaimed PROUD TO BE AN AMERICAN. I saw that his keys were held together by an American flag key chain that still had the tag on them.

Now I understood. Terror looked like this.

"If they reach in that bag, I know something," a young black man wearing green wristbands said to his friend.

"What you know?" I asked.

"I know they better not try to blow up this train," he said, loud enough so everyone in our car could hear. "That's what I know."

A white man whose chest hair looked like it was soaked in curl activator nodded affirmatively across the aisle from us and gave the young brother a thumbs-up. "USA, right?" the white man asked.

"You already know," he shot back. "USA."

I rolled my eyes. "These white folk got you tripping," I whispered for the family in front of me to hear, and then added more loudly, for everyone, "These people ain't trying to blow up no train."

For the entire hour to Grand Central Terminal, the family in front of me sat still and erect, rarely tilting their heads to speak to each other. Every time the child, who looked like he was six or seven, tried to move, his parents held him in place. For the first time in my life, I experienced not having the most fear-provoking body in a contained American space. Of course, folks on that train were still afraid of black bodies like mine, but they were more afraid of brown folks who "looked" like Muslims. I kept thinking of your directive to be excellent, disciplined, elegant, emotionally contained, clean, and perfect in the face of American white supremacy. "I gotta pee," the boy whispered to his mother, but she wouldn't let go of his arm.

When the train pulled into Grand Central, the father grabbed their suitcase from the bin and the boy stood next to his parents. The mother placed her body and the suitcase in front of the child, shielding our eyes from his piss-darkened red shorts.

"Thank you," the mother said as she walked by me.

"You're welcome," I said. "Y'all have a good day."

I wondered if this feeling I had was what "good white folk" felt when we thanked them for not being as terrible as they could be.

As I walked deeper into New York City that day, I saw and heard black, brown, and white men in a Lower East Side bodega filled with mini American flags talk about harming "the Moozlums who blew up our city" and speculate about where they would attack next.

183

Thirty minutes later, I stood dizzy in a cathedral near Ground Zero, passing out bottled water, sandwiches, and blankets to tired firefighters still looking for survivors. For the first time since I left you six years earlier, I knew you and Grandmama were safer back in Jackson than I was up north. Your safety had nothing to do with airplanes torpedoing skyscrapers filled with people just doing their jobs. Y'all were safer because you knew exactly where you were in the world.

I'd been forced, since I left you in that driveway six years earlier, to accept I didn't understand much about any part of the country other than our part of Mississippi. I assumed all black folk in the nation were from the Deep South. I had no idea how many black folk there were in the nation from Africa and the Caribbean.

That day in lower Manhattan, inside the cathedral, you would have seen so much generosity and patience in the face of absolute fear and loss. Before leaving, we held little American flags, gripped coarse American hands, and thanked each other for bringing the best of our American selves out to help. I assumed, though, everyone in that loving space knew what was going to happen next. I didn't know much about New York, but I knew what white Americans demanded of America. White Americans, primarily led by George W. Bush, were about to wrap themselves in flags and chant "USA!" as poor cousins, friends, sons, and daughters showed a weaker, browner, less Christian part of the world how *we* dealt with loss.

When I took the train back to Poughkeepsie that night, I remember feeling sad there were no "Muslim-looking" folk in my car whom I could feel good about defending. I imagined the looks of awe on the faces of my students when I told them I volunteered. I looked out at the Hudson River and thanked God the attacks of 9/11 hadn't happened while a black president was in office. I wondered, for the first time in my life, what being an American, not just a black American from Mississippi, really demanded of my insides, and what the consequences were for not meeting that demand in the world.

I waited in the parking lot of my apartment for a white woman walking out of the complex to get in her car so I wouldn't scare her. On the way into my apartment, I saw and heard an airplane. I remembered some of the Jamaican men in an NYC bodega talking about a nuclear facility thirty miles from me called Indian Point. According to them, Muslims were going to fly four planes into Indian Point in the next few days, causing hundreds of thousands of Americans to die from acute radiation syndrome and cancer.

I ran into my apartment, called you, called Grandmama, did some push-ups, weighed myself, ran six miles, came back home, locked the bedroom door, did more push-ups, got in bed, and listened for loud booms brought on by terrifying Muslim-looking folk who supposedly hated us because of our freedom.

A few months later, a senior white colleague suggested I direct Cole's thesis. Cole was one of his thesis advisees who lost people close to him on September 11. He told me he was sure I "could connect with Cole" in ways he couldn't. While I appreciated Cole's dirty fingernails and the reckless way he went after loose balls during pickup basketball games, I never had Cole as a student. Cole, whose thesis was on Dante's *Inferno*, was a slim, wealthy, Jewish white boy from Connecticut who'd wrestled addiction since he was a sophomore in high school.

Cole and I spent hours in my office that semester, pushing through theories of immersion in Dante's *Inferno* on Wednesdays and talking through his experiences of abandonment and addiction on Fridays. In addition to talking to me, Cole made use of the counseling services on campus, and a private counselor off campus.

One day when Cole was leaving my office, Heedy "Douglass" Byers, whom I was introduced to by my friend Brown, was waiting outside my door. Folk in Poughkeepsie called Heedy "Douglass" because he had a blown-out Afro and a massive combed-in part like Frederick Douglass. Douglass called me "Keys" and he said it at the beginning and ends of his sentences. As Cole and Douglass passed each other, I watched them make *that* exchange I'd seen hundreds of times in Jackson, Forest, Oberlin, and Bloomington.

I pulled Douglass into my office after Cole turned the corner, and closed the door while six black, South Asian, and Filipina students waited outside my office. "You moving shit right in front of my office like that?"

"Keys," he said. "If you ever need anything, trust me. I got you, Keys. Whatever you need, let me know, Keys. You and Brown trying to ball after work?"

I taught two courses a semester for eighteen thousand dollars a year after taxes. Even though you and Aunt Linda made more money, I somehow had more disposable income than anyone in our family. When I got my job, I imagined doing all kinds of stuff with my new money, like going to IHOP once a week, buying three new albums, three new books every month, and buying a new pair of Adidas at the end of every semester.

It didn't take me long to realize my eighteen thousand a year wasn't close to rich, especially when you told me you needed eleven hundred for the air conditioner, four hundred to fix the plumbing, and three hundred for new tires on the car. That same day Cole and Douglass made the exchange, you called and asked me if I could send eight hundred dollars home for Grandmama's new dental bridge. You said she was in excruciating pain and she was too proud to ask me for the money. I told you I would send all the money I could by the end of the week.

"I love you, Kie," you said. "Thank you for always helping the family when we need it."

When I got off the phone, Douglass looked at my fingers lightly tapping the faded wood on the desk. I watched him watch the mountains of books covering the wall, the peeling blue Baldwin poster behind my door, a vinyl version of Jay Z's *Blueprint*, the warped picture of Grandmama holding her chin on the windowsill. "Keys, what you wanna do, Keys. You wanna invest in this work?"

Ever since I was twelve, I was surrounded by Mississippi black boys for whom slanging was a side hustle. My friends didn't call themselves "hustlers" or "dope boys." They were black boys who wanted to augment money earned at primary jobs by selling a product that made people feel better about being alive. Lots of us were grandchildren of hardworking bootlegging grandparents who shared the importance of multiple side hustles and varied streams of income. So even if we slang, we were going to deliver phone books, bus tables at Applebee's, mow someone's lawn, or teach.

It wasn't complicated.

You, Uncle Jimmy, and Boots from the Coup convinced me drugs distorted our work ethic, weakening our body's ability to imagine, resist, organize, and remember. You claimed that weakened bodies and weakened imaginations made us easier prey for white supremacy. I didn't disagree with you but I never knocked my friends' side hustles. All I ever said was, "The longer you slang, the higher the likelihood white folk gone hem you up."

None of us were the grandchildren of grandparents who passed money or land down to our parents. Even those of us whose parents were part of this shiny black middle class knew those shiny black middle-class parents were one paycheck away from asking grandparents or us for money we didn't have the week before payday, and two paychecks away from poverty. There was no wealth in our family, you told me more than once. There were only paydays.

By nineteen, when I finally accepted Uncle Jimmy's addiction, I decided that if I ever slang, I'd only slang to white folk. By twenty, I realized there wasn't one white person on earth I trusted with my freedom. The problem with slanging to white folk was that, rich or poor, they already had way too much influence on whether we ended up in prison or dead. Giving white folk even more of that absolute power always felt like side hustling backward.

Still, thinking about the inflamed nerves in Grandmama's mouth, and knowing you needed more money for some reason almost every week, I wondered if this was the one time in my life I could get away with "collaborating." Douglass told me a few weeks after we met that he "collaborated" with other Dutchess County professors in endeavors that were "financially beneficial to both sides, Keys."

I asked him if any of those professor collaborators were black.

"Not yet, Keys," he said. "Not yet. You could be the first." When Douglass left my office, waiting outside were Adam, Niki, Bama, Ghislaine, Matt, and Mazie. Instead of coming into the office one at a time, my black and brown students often came in together and sat in a half circle. Nearly all of the students who made a second home during my office hours had been targeted, disciplined, exceptionalized, and fetishized because of their race, gender, and/or sexuality, in and out of classrooms, on and off campus. They dealt with neo-Nazi groups targeting them, antiblack iconography etched on walls; some got suspended and expelled for infractions white students were rarely even written up for; campus security and local police routinely questioned their identities and the identities of their guests.

Three hours after my students walked in, they all walked out of my office except for Mazie, a tall, queer black girl from Arkansas. Mazie's talent as a writer and scholar were frightening. A semester earlier, Mazie was kicked out of school for allegedly threatening her roommate after she disrespected Mazie's mama. I served as Mazie's faculty support during her hearing. When the judicial board suspended Mazie, we protested and appealed the suspension. Mazie was allowed back on campus but not allowed in the library or dorms after dark. I knew, after Mazie's suspension, I needed to get on that judicial board to make sure what happened to Mazie never happened to another vulnerable student.

After an hour and a half, the sun started to go down and I told Mazie I should probably go get ready for this student judicial hearing.

I turned the light off and walked out behind her. "You friends with that white boy, Cole?" she asked me in the parking lot.

"Friends? Nah. He's my thesis student."

"Good. That white boy and his friends, they be slangin' so much of that shit on this campus."

"How you know?"

"I just know," she said, before dapping me up and walking toward Main Building.

I thought about the older colleague who suggested I work with Cole, the same colleague who insisted on letting me know how lucky I was every time he saw me. He had no idea what my work was on, no idea what I wanted to do with language, no idea who or what I was before getting a job at Vassar. We both knew Cole, a dealer of everything from weed to cocaine, could be a college graduate, college professor, college trustee, or president of all kinds of American things in spite of being scared, desperate, and guilty.

By my third semester at Vassar, I learned it was fashionable to call Cole's predicament "privilege" and not "power." I had the privilege of being raised by you and a grandmama who responsibly loved me in the blackest, most creative state in the nation. Cole had the power to never be poor and never be a felon, the power to always have his failures treated as success no matter how mediocre he was. Cole's power necessitated he literally was too white, too masculine, too rich to fail. George Bush was president because of Cole's power. An even richer, more mediocre white man could be president next because of Cole's power. Even progressive presidents would bow to Cole's power. Grandmama, the smartest, most responsible human being I knew, cut open chicken bellies and washed the shit out of white folks' dirty underwear because of Cole's power. She could never be president. And she never wanted to be because she knew that the job necessitated moral mediocrity. My job, I learned that first year, was to dutifully teach Cole to use this power less abusively. I was supposed to encourage Cole to understand his power brought down buildings, destroyed countries, created prisons, and lathered itself in blood and suffering. But if used for good, his power could lay the foundation for liberation and some greater semblance of justice in our country, and possibly the world.

I just didn't buy it.

I loved my job, and I understood the first week of school it was impossible to teach any student you despised. A teacher's job was to responsibly love the students in front of them. If I was doing my job, I had to find a way to love the wealthy white boys I taught with the same integrity with which I loved my black students, even if the constitution of that love differed. This wasn't easy because no matter how conscientious, radically curious, or politically active I encouraged Cole to be, teaching wealthy white boys like him meant I was being paid to really fortify Cole's power.

In return for this care, I'd get a monthly check, some semblance of security, and moral certainty we were helping white folk be better at being human. This was new to me, but it was old black work, and this old black work, in ways you warned me about, was more than selling out; this old black work was morally side hustling backward.

The judicial case we were tasked with looking at that night was sad and simple like most of the cases we heard. Security came into Cole's best friend's dorm room. They saw and took pictures of felonious amounts of cocaine, little scales, and Baggies on the table. Cole's best friend, a small, smart white boy with massive eyebrows, was being charged with possession and intent to distribute. I never really understood how or why college judicial boards were hearing potential felony cases, but I had more trust in the college judicial boards to fairly adjudicate these situations than actual jails, judges, juries, police, and prisons.

During the small, smart white boy's opening statement, he talked about being at a club in the city of Poughkeepsie and being approached by a "big dark man" who made him buy cocaine. I sat back in my chair and looked around the room. Everyone in the room was white. And every white person in the room was transfixed by the story of the small, smart white boy being made to buy cocaine by a nigger on the floor of a club in Poughkeepsie. I breathed heavy through the student's opening statement, through security's statement, and through the student's closing statement. I kept thinking of Brown, the first person I met in Poughkeepsie. He was in prison for violating parole, and he went to prison the first few times for selling less coke than was found in this small, smart white boy's room. I thought about how even when we weren't involved in selling drugs, big, dark folks like us could be used to shield white folk from responsibility.

Brown was five-seven, 220 pounds. Big and dark.

I was six-one, 179 pounds. Big and dark.

Mazie was five-nine, 158 pounds. Big and dark.

I'd looked like a big, dark black man since I was an eleven-year-old black boy. I'd been surrounded by big, dark black men since I was born. I never met one big, dark black man who would make a white boy buy cocaine. Apparently, there was one such big, dark black man in Poughkeepsie, New York.

The rest of the disciplinary committee said we couldn't

hold the small, smart white boy responsible for possession because the details of what led to his possession of cocaine were so frightening. We don't know what it's like to be as small as this kid, the professor next to me said, and be forced to buy coke from a scary person in a downtown club.

"We don't?" I asked him.

We don't know what it's like to go through what he went through, another administrator said.

I asked both of them why any man who could make a person buy cocaine would not just take the person's money and keep his cocaine. The professor started talking to me about transformative justice. I told him that I knew well what transformative justice was, and asked again how anything transformative could be happening in this room if it's predicated on us believing a big black dude made the small, smart white boy buy cocaine.

Everyone in the room looked at me like I had hog-head cheese oozing out of my nose. He never said the guy was black, another member of the committee said. If the small, smart white boy did not technically possess the cocaine, the small, smart white boy could not be held responsible for intent to distribute cocaine. If the small, smart white boy was found not responsible for distributing cocaine, he would have to be let free.

No expulsion.

No suspension.

No disciplinary probation.

I kept looking at the black-and-white pictures of felonious amounts of cocaine, the scale, the Baggies. Apparently, I did not see what I saw because a big black man in the city of Poughkeepsie, a nigger, made me see it.

I didn't have my own computer or Internet at home, so I walked back to my office after the hearing to e-mail Cole. I believed in prison abolition. But I wasn't sure how fair it was to practice transformative justice on the cisgendered, hetero-sexual, white, rich male body of someone who'd been granted transformative justice since birth. I didn't want Cole making a home in my office anymore. I didn't want his little skinny white self talking to me about drugs he'd never be guilty of consuming or selling in Poughkeepsie. I asked Cole over e-mail if we could meet in the library from now on.

I leaned back in my chair and looked at my office.

I picked up a chewed pen, a green spiral notebook, and I wrote the names of every person I knew in jail or prison for drug-related offenses. I filled that white piece of paper with black friends, black cousins, black uncles, and black aunties. Some of those black names were serving upwards of thirty years in prison for far less cocaine than the small, smart white boy who was forced to buy cocaine in a club. Then I wrote the names of young people I met in Poughkeepsie who were locked up for drug-related offenses.

Cole responded to my e-mail a few minutes later, say-ing he'd really appreciate it if we kept meeting in my office because it was the only place he felt safe on that campus.

"That's fine," I wrote, "if that's what you want to do."

I threw my notebook across my office, yelled "mother-fucker," and texted Douglass.

This Keys. I ain't doing that thing. We ballin at 8 tomorrow if you can make it. I can scoop you.

I didn't want to waste any of my phone's minutes so I used the department business code to call you back before leaving my office. I told you I was sorry for waking you up and asked if I could wire half of the money this month and half of the money next month.

"Thank you," you said. "Wire what you can tomorrow, Kie. Please know that we need it as soon as possible."

I hung up the phone, grabbed my keys, unlocked the English faculty lounge, and stole some colleagues' Fresca, a blueberry-vanilla yogurt, and granola from the office fridge. I left my car at work, ran to my apartment, did some push-ups, weighed myself, ran six miles around Poughkeepsie, came back home, locked the bedroom door, did more push-ups, said prayers, got in bed, and accepted no matter how much weight I lost, small, smart white boys would always have the power to make big black boys force them into buying our last kilos of cocaine. Then some of us would watch them watch us watch them walk free after getting caught. And some of us, if we were extra lucky, would get to teach these small, smart, addicted white boys and girls today so we could pay for our ailing grandmamas' dental care tomorrow.

SEAT BELTS

You were on your way to Vassar from Cuba, while I was 0.7 pounds away from 165 pounds after playing two hours of basketball, running eleven miles, eating three PowerBars, and drinking two gallons of water a day. The fourth day of my seventh semester at Vassar, I bought a used stair-stepper from the gym. After three more hours of basketball, and an hour of jogging, I maxed the heat in my tiny apartment and stair-stepped until I was down to 165.7 pounds, sixty pounds less than I weighed at twelve years old, and 153.3 pounds less than I weighed at my heaviest. The heaviest version of my body was past tense. My current body was present tense. There was no limit to how light I could be, and I knew I needed to live in the future.

I had 2.5 percent body fat the day I picked you up from the train station in Poughkeepsie.

In the past six years, you'd worked in over fifteen countries. You were paid little to nothing for these work trips, and you still had a full-time professor and associate dean job, but you said the trips made living in Mississippi and the United States bearable. You looked around at empty buildings in downtown Poughkeepsie. You watched Oaxacans and black folk walking down main street and said for the first time in my life, "I'm so glad you left home. I think you'd like Cuba."

"You hate Mississippi and America, huh?"

"I don't hate Mississippi, Kie," you said. "I don't hate America. I hate the backlash that happens anytime black folk strive to make our state better than its origins. Sometimes I think Mississippi is home to the greatest and the worst people ever created."

"Yeah," I said. "I think the same thing about America as a whole."

"Do you think you'll ever travel abroad?" you asked me. "I think you'd appreciate the work I do in Cuba, Zimbabwe, Palestine, and Romania."

I sucked my teeth, laughed, and reminded you I was afraid of flying and asked you not to ever say the word "abroad" in my car or apartment. You started laughing and told me to get a grip.

The whole first day you were in my apartment, you kept asking what my father, who visited me a few weeks earlier, said about you. Eventually, I lied and said he asked about your work. When you asked me if he seemed proud of you, I lied again and said yes.

The truth was that when my father walked his five feet eight inches, 250 pounds into my office, he closed his eyes and said, "I'm so proud of you, son." I told him I had to meet with some students before we could leave so he sat outside my office on a bench. My father sat with nothing in his hands. No books. No magazines. No cell phone. He just looked up at the empty bookcases in the waiting area and wouldn't stop smiling.

After office hours, he went with me to the gym and watched me warm up by running a few miles on the track. Then he sat on the floor, with his back against the maroon mat, while I practiced with the basketball team. Twenty minutes after we got there, my father was asleep.

When we got in my car, my father didn't put on his seat belt. He kept looking out the passenger window at the stars. "I'm so proud of you, son," he said again as I took him to get a salad.

I offered my father my bed when we got home to my four-hundred-square-foot apartment but he refused. He told me again how proud he was of me for not quitting after getting kicked out of college. No matter what he was talking about, every few minutes he looked at my chest, forearms, neck, and legs and said, "You look great, Kie. I'm really proud of how you're taking care of yourself."

When my father said he thought I was ready to hear a story he should have told me years ago, I thought he was going to tell me something about you. Instead, he told me how a white sheriff in Enterprise, Mississippi, raped his mother, my grandma Pudding, when he was a child. My father said the sheriff neglected the child born from the rape, and threw my grandfather Tom in prison for two years for bootlegging when some white teenagers crashed after purchasing his product. My father wanted me to know he suspected his little brother, the child of the rape, was killed by someone he knew when he was a baby, as was the sheriff who raped his mother. More than solving the mystery of who killed his little brother or the sheriff, my father wanted me to understand that the so-called terror linking all Americans was nothing compared to the racial and gendered terror that controlled and contorted the bodies of our family.

"It is not theoretical, Kie," he tried to tell me that night. "None of it. That's why I'm so proud of you. They came after you like they came after both sides of your family. Your mother and I went about fighting that terror differently. I fought my fight from the inside of corporate America. You and your mother fought it through education."

I never understood why black dudes who worked for corporations called their employers "corporate America" no matter if they were CEOs, members of the janitorial staff, or seasonal temporary workers.

Anyway, that was the only time my father mentioned you. Then he started talking about his trips to Vegas and asked me if I ever thought about going out there with him. When I asked him if he ever missed you, his big eyes started closing, so I went in the bathroom, did some push-ups, threw some punches in the mirror, and got in the shower. When I got out, my father was slumped over with both feet on the floor, glasses still on, one fist balled up on his lap, one hand tucked under his left thigh.

"I wish I had a professor like you when I was in school," my father said as I covered him in the orange-red quilt you gave me for Christmas. My father didn't come to Poughkeepsie to tell me something I already knew about the familial impact of racial terror in our nation. He didn't come to tell me something I suspected about the violation of his mother and his brother. He was running, ducking, deflecting, and he didn't want to run, duck, or deflect anymore. I felt all of what he told me, but I knew there was more his body needed to say.

That night, I saw in that slumping, sleeping black man the ten-year-old black child who ran away from home because he tired of the beatings his father gave his mother and siblings. I saw the fourteen-year-old black child charged with hiding the money his father made from bootlegging. I saw the sixteen-year-old black child forced to share his valedictorian honor with a white student with a lower GPA. I saw the nineteen-year-old black child who sold weed to make it through college. I saw the twenty-year-old black child who proudly repped the Republic of New Afrika. I saw the twenty-one-year-old black child who loved to have sex but hated talking about love with his wife. I saw the twenty-seven-year-old black child who sent his son and ex-wife postcards every week.

I'd never given much weight to the idea of present black fathers saving black boys. Most of the black boys I grew up with had present black fathers in the home. Sure, some of those fathers taught my friends how to be tough. But I can't think of one who encouraged his son to be emotionally or even bodily expressive of joy, fear, and love. I respected my father but I never felt that I needed him or any other man in the house to show me how to become a loving man. I knew, truth be told, that a present American man would likely teach me how to be a present American man. And I couldn't imagine how those teachings would have made me healthier or more generous. What I saw of my father that day didn't make me miss the father who was rarely present in my childhood, but it made me feel the beautiful black boy you fell in love with. It reaffirmed my belief that you needed a loving partner in our home far more than I needed a present father. I realized you and my father had broken and you'd never tell anyone about the depth of the breaks.

And all of that made me miss you.

Instead of telling you any of that, I asked you why you had so many questions about someone you don't even know anymore. "We have a child together, Kie. We knew each other. We'll always know each other." When I said okay, you asked more about both of his marriages and the young children he had with his third wife.

"It's all good," I told you. "Everything with him is all good. I don't ask questions. I don't get answers."

My schedule of running at least six miles during the day and six miles at night didn't work when you were in Poughkeepsie. You worried too much the police would shoot me, so I couldn't leave the house after midnight. I told you I ran at night to help process workdays.

"You have to find some way to deal with the stress of doing this job that doesn't involve the possibility of you getting shot."

"How is running at night increasing the possibility of my getting shot?"

"Please," you said. "You are a big black man. Stop running at night." I asked you if you still thought I was big even though I had hardly any body fat. "To white folk and police, you will always be huge no matter how skinny you are. Get a grip."

The morning you were scheduled to leave, we took a picture on one of the lawns at Vassar. I didn't want to take the picture because I felt so fat. I wore a stained red shirt and jeans I wished were looser. You threw on your shades, and I cocked my head back. That red, white, green, blue, and brown picture was the last picture we'd ever take together.

Before I dropped you off at the train station, you took me to the furniture store and bought me a two-thousand-dollar living room set that I begged you not to buy. Then you asked about my father again and congratulated me on my body. "It took a lot of work to get a strong, fine body like that," you said. "You've got the body your father had when I met him. Remember those tiny shorts he would wear?"

I didn't want to talk to you about my father's tiny shorts.

"Thanks," I said instead. "I guess."

"You love your students so much, Kie. That's something I think you got from me. I'm glad y'all have each other. It makes me worry about you less up here."

"I don't think I love my students in healthy ways," I told you. "I don't think I know how."

Four days later, you called and asked me to send twenty-five hundred dollars for a medicine your state insurance didn't cover. I didn't even ask what it was for. I just wired the money, and waited for the now twenty-five-hundred-dollar leather living room set I didn't want to be delivered in the first place.

I spent the next few months in my classroom, in office hours, writing, exercising, taking care of students, and sending you more money. I'd gone from teaching three courses at Vassar to teaching six to being offered a job there on the tenure track. A month after I was put on the tenure track, you left to do more work in Cuba. I was the only one in the family who knew you'd gone. You didn't want Grandmama to worry. You called me as soon as you made it back. Instead of telling me about your trip, you told me the fireplace in the house was decaying and the house needed a new foundation as soon as possible. You said squirrels infested the house and you could hear them running through the kitchen at night.

"Ain't nothing in that kitchen for them to eat," I told you, "unless they eating spoiled buttermilk and old Bisquick."

"The man is in there fixing the fireplace now," you said, "but I don't have enough money to pay him. Can you wire a thousand dollars, Kie? I need five hundred for the fireplace and five hundred for a new furnace."

"Can I speak to him?"

"What did you say? You're breaking up."

"Can I speak to the person fixing the place?" I asked you. "Maybe I can get him to lower his price."

The phone went dead.

I called you back. There was no answer.

I called Grandmama and asked her if you could stay with her until the fireplace got fixed, since squirrels were running through the house.

"What kind of squirrels and thangs you talking about, Kie?"

"I heard there were squirrels all in the house because the chimney cracked."

"Naw," Grandmama said, "I was over to Jackson yesterday and I ain't see no squirrels. The air wasn't working and the plumbing was broken, but wasn't no squirrels and thangs running around. What in the world is you talking about?"

"That's what I'm asking you," I said. "How can the plumbing and air be broken when I sent her money for that a few weeks ago?"

"Kie." Grandmama held the pause. "Kie, listen to me. That house is crumbling around her and something in this milk ain't clean. You hear me? Somebody stole my checkbook, my credit cards, the little money I had in my closet, too. I wasn't gonna say nothing about it, but this is getting ridiculous."

"What are you talking about? Who is somebody?"

"I'm talking about don't let somebody play you for no fool. God give you five senses for a reason."

I closed my flip phone and sat on the tacky leather couch. Since working at Vassar, I gave you tens of thousands of dollars for mortgages, engines, groceries, and doctor bills. Sometimes I contacted the places you owed and paid them directly.

I never asked myself how someone who made twice as much as I made could be broke the second week into every month. I didn't care. You'd taken care of me for half of my life, and I wanted, as much as I could, to take care of you. But I wasn't rich. And I just wanted to know where my money was going if it wasn't going where you said it was.

You called me back from the grocery store and told me to wire the money immediately. I told you that something felt strange and I didn't feel right wiring money without talking to the person I was supposedly paying. I'd just given you the fourteen thousand dollars I had in savings for a down payment on an SUV you said would make you feel safer, and if I was going to send you another thousand, I just needed to know we were getting the best deal we could get.

You hung up in my face again.

I called you back, but you still wouldn't answer. I told your voice mail I could send more money but I needed to know what I was sending money for. I didn't tell your voice mail Grandmama said somebody stole her money. I didn't tell your voice mail I was starving myself, or that I was in the midst of confusing teaching with parenting and befriending and loving. "Please call me back," I said.

I put on my shoes, took off my shirt, and told my body I was going to run twenty miles that night. My body did not want to run twenty miles that night because it played three hours of ball and ran six miles earlier. My body wanted water. It wanted its first good night's sleep in five years. It wanted more than a thousand calories. I ignored what my body wanted because nothing my body wanted would get me beneath 160 pounds.

Twenty-three miles later, I limped in the house drenched in

sweat, buzzing from endorphins. I stepped heavy on the scale and watched the number get smaller and smaller.

290.

275.

250.

225.

205.

190.

183.

175.

165.

159.3.

I was the lightest I'd ever been since I was nine years old. I checked my messages, hoping you'd called me back. You had not. I took a shower and sat on my bed. When I went to get up and call you again, I could not stand. The blood in my left leg, from the top of my ass to the tip of my big toe, felt like it was boiling. I told myself if I drank water and just fell asleep on the floor, I would recover.

I woke up three hours later. I had not recovered. The tenses in my body were colliding.

The following day was the first day in 2,564 days I didn't run at least six miles. I hopped myself over to my scale. I weighed 163 pounds. I tried to burn calories by hopping a mile on my right foot, but just holding my left leg off the ground was unbearable. I didn't know how I could sweat enough to get me back below 160 if I could not walk. I kept calling you but you wouldn't answer the phone.

I lay on the floor of that tiny apartment listening to tenses in my body. I couldn't feel the toes on my left foot. My left hip socket felt like it was being eaten out by fire ants. That

Thursday, the first day in eight years I did not push my body to exhaustion, my body knew what was going to happen, because it, and only it, knew what I'd made it do, and what I hoped it would forget. I sat on the floor knowing my body broke because I carried and created secrets that were way too heavy.

My body knew in three weeks I would still be unable to walk. It knew I would punish it for not being able to walk by eating cheese sticks and honey buns until I weighed 184 pounds. It knew at 184 pounds, I'd call it a fat piece of shit over and over again, and I would eventually take it to the doctor, hoping the doctor would fix it so I could run it into exhaustion again.

After taking all kinds of tests, it knew the doctor would tell me in addition to the herniated disks, the sciatica, the massive scar tissue in my left ankle and knee from fractures, sprains, and overuse, I had some abnormal cell growth that contributed to the deterioration of my hip socket. My body knew the doctor would give me a prescription and another appointment, suggest therapy, and say I needed surgery that would keep me off my legs for at least three to four months.

My body knew I would make appointments for the procedure and therapy, but skip them both. It knew I would gorge it for weeks until I was 206 pounds, and feel heavier at 206 than I felt at 319 pounds. At 206, it knew I would cancel everything I was supposed to show up to on campus except class. When I showed up, my colleagues and students would ask me if I was okay. My body would remember when I had 3 percent body fat, ran thirteen miles a day, ate vegan, had lots of visible veins, and fainted a lot. It would remember taking off my shirt and shoes in the weight room to weigh myself surrounded by thin women people secretly called anorexic

and bulimic. It would remember never worrying about anyone calling me anorexic or bulimic though I was the first one
at the gym at six in the morning and the last one to leave at
ten. Like nearly everyone else at the gym, I wasn't in the gym
to be healthy, I was in the gym to feel in control of how fat I
looked and felt.

My body knew that my weight, the exact number, became
an emotional, psychological, and spiritual destination a long
time ago. I knew, and worried, about how much I weighed
and exactly how much money I had every day of my life since
I was eleven years old. The weight reminded me of how much
I'd eaten, how much I'd starved, how much I'd exercised, and
how much I sat still yesterday. My body knew I was no more
liberated or free when I was 159 pounds with 2 percent body
fat than I was at 319 pounds with achy joints. I loved the rush
of pushing my body beyond places it never wanted to go, but
I was addicted to controlling the number on that scale. Controlling that number on the scale, more than writing a story
or essay or feeling loved or making money or having sex,
made me feel less gross, and most abundant. Losing weight
helped me forget.

When I weighed over two hundred pounds again, I would
not touch my body. I would not want anyone else to touch my
body. I would not believe anyone who knew me when I was
159 could love me or want to touch me when I was over two
hundred pounds. As the number continued to climb, I would
teach and I would write and I would revise, and I would avoid
you and Grandmama. I would continue to lie to the one person
in the world who did everything she could to make sure I was
healthy. I would learn fifteen years too late that asking for consent, granting consent, surviving sexual violence, being called

a good dude, and never initiating sexual relationships did not incubate me from being emotionally abusive. Consent meant little to nothing if it was not fully informed. What, and to whom, were my partners consenting if I spent our entire relationship convincing them that a circle was not a circle but just a really relaxed square? I'd become good at losing weight and great at convincing women they didn't see or know what they absolutely saw and knew. Lying there on that floor, I accepted that I'd actually never been honest in any relationship in my life, and I'd never been honest with myself about what carrying decades of lies did to other people's hearts and heads.

I would stop talking to you because I did not know how to say no, and everything I said yes to was a lie. But you would not stop reaching out, particularly when you thought our bodies and our homes were in danger. When the levees broke and Katrina obliterated the coast of Mississippi, and President Bush neglected our folks because they were black, poor, and southern, you would tell your 209-pound child that our cousins made it out of New Orleans and they were sleeping in my bedroom. A few years later, we would meet a skinny, scared, scarred, brilliant black man who walked like you want me to walk, talked like you want me to talk, and wrote like you want me write. When he became president of the United States, you would tell your 235-pound child that the costs of any president loving black folks might be too much, but the violent white backlash to Obama's victory will still be unlike anything we'd ever seen. We will pay the cost of his election now and later, I would hear you say over and over again.

At 314 pounds, I should have told you that I was sitting in a room in Main Building with a senior professor and two high-ranking administrators. I would come to the meeting with a contraption under my shirt that measures the irregularities of my heartbeat. The committee tasked with reviewing my tenure file first asked for an unredacted contract for my first book after the president told them not to ask for it. They then mistakingly sent my colleague, Flora Wadley, who had the same initials as a member of the committee—an e-mail insinuating I was lying about my graduation from grad school. Near the end of the meeting, this white senior professor on the committee affirmed their white liberal commitment to "African Americans" and said members of the committee believed I was a "fraud."

I would tuck both hands underneath my buttocks as tears pooled in the gutters of both eyes. I would come into that meeting knowing the illest part of racial terror in this nation is that it's sanctioned by sorry, overpaid white bodies that will never be racially terrorized, and maintained by a few desperate underpaid black and brown bodies that will. I would leave that meeting knowing that there are few things more shameful than being treated like a nigger by—and under the gaze of—intellectually and imaginatively average white Americans who are not, and will never have to be, half as good at their jobs as you are at yours.

Neither that day, nor the day I was stuck on the floor, hoping you'd answer the phone, would I have the will to imagine the night a detective from Poughkeepsie asks my 319-pound body to come by the precinct. I'd been to the police station in Poughkeepsie on four different occasions helping students, and seven other times to pay traffic violations. Two members of the tenure committee, and another senior professor, will receive anonymous racist, sexist, anti-Semitic letters threatening them for what they did to me. The professors will turn the letters over to the Poughkeepsie police, and a detective will call me into the station at ten o'clock Monday night.

I will walk into the interrogation room and watch the detective ask me if I knew who could have sent the threatening letters. I will explain, as best I can, that no one who had my best interest in heart would threaten folk on a disgraced tenure committee with anti-Semitic, racist, sexist language.

"I hear you," he will say. "We have a suspect."

"Who is it?"

"I'm looking at him," he will say and ask me if I'd be willing to take a polygraph test.

"I'll take that shit right now."

"Really?"

"Yeah," I will suck my teeth. "Really."

I will understand that I am a heavy black boy from Mississippi, which means that I am vulnerable. But unlike most heavy black boys from Mississippi, I have a solid check coming in every month for the rest of my life. I have "professor" associated with my name. I have a mother and father with almost powerful friends who could help defend me if I needed it. I will understand that I am vulnerable but I am not powerless. I am not powerless because, though we have no wealth, we have peculiar access to something resembling black power.

I will question what we had to give up to get this peculiar access to something resembling black power when the detective says, "I'm just doing my job." He will ask me if I think he wants to be wasting my time with stupid professor beefs at Vassar College with all the drugs and violence in Dutchess County?

I will tell him there are a lot of drugs and violence at Vassar College, too.

The detective will walk out of the interrogation room, and

I will sit there looking at the handcuffs on the table in front of me. I will wonder how coming up for tenure at Vassar College landed me in an interrogation room. All I will want to do is run.

Not to my apartment.

Not to a classroom.

Not to my office.

Not to deceitful sex.

Not to you.

The detective will come back into the room and tell me they plan on contacting me tomorrow about the polygraph test. Tomorrow will come and the detective will never call. When I call him, he will tell me they no longer need me to take the test. I will not know if that meant they found who actually sent the letters or if they did not want to extend any more resources on threats made against the professors making the accusations, or if the detective was intentionally agitating me all along.

Either way, I am supposed to be happy because I am free, because I am not in handcuffs, because I have peculiar access to something resembling black power. I will know that I am not free precisely because I am happy that my wrists are free of handcuffs the month I earn tenure with distinction from Vassar College.

That Thursday, six years before I end up in an interrogation room for coming up for tenure, the first day in eight years I did not push my body to exhaustion, my body knew what was going to happen, because it, and only it, knew what I'd made it do and what I'd hoped it would forget.

I am sprawled out on the floor of my apartment, looking at the shiny brown leather couch. I call you again and hope you answer so I can tell you, for the first time in my life, that I need your help. I want to ask you if you remember the day you drove me to Grandmama's house when I was twelve years old. Before picking me up to take me, I tried calling you at your office and I let the phone ring for twenty-three minutes. When you finally came, you drove me to Grandmama's because you thought Grandmama could fix me. We were expecting my father's child support payment but you told me it hadn't come yet because the mail carrier might have stolen it.

When we pulled off on the Forest exit to the right of Interstate 20, we came to a stop sign. We made our way left onto Highway 35. Neither of us looked to our right at the tractor-trailer roaring toward the passenger side of the Nova. The truck driver pummeled the horn. You floored the brakes of the Nova, slung your right arm across my body even though you made me put on my seat belt before we left Jackson. Since you were not wearing your seat belt, your chest smashed into the steering wheel. I was four inches taller than you, and at least thirty pounds heavier than you at that point, but I didn't try to secure you. I asked if you were okay before my body reached across your body to put on your seat belt. You told me you loved me as we headed down Old Morton Road to Grandmama's house. I told you I loved you, too. We meant different things, but we meant I love you.

"It's me again," I say into your voice mail from the floor of my apartment. I am naked, holding my hip with my left hand, and holding my flip phone with my right. "Can you just call me back so I know you're okay? I'll be here waiting for you to call when you get ready. I won't ask what happened to the money. I think something is really wrong with my body. Can you help me?"

PROMISES

You were sitting in front of a slot machine in Connecticut, looking nervously over both shoulders, while I was hiding fifteen feet behind you with ten dollars I'd stolen from Flora Wadley's apartment in my back pocket. I had no idea how much I weighed. I just knew it felt like well over 320 pounds or well under 165 pounds.

We were both so far from home. You quit your job at Jackson State and moved just three and a half hours from Poughkeepsie and one and a half hours from the casino. Every weekend, you asked me to visit you. Every weekend I said no. I realized four years earlier you weren't doing with my money what you said you were doing. I didn't know how to be around you and not give you whatever you wanted. I wasn't trying to punish you. I was trying to do less harm to myself. I never visited you, but I saw you so many times in that casino playing your same machine, looking nervously over your left and right shoulder the way you did the first time I saw you win in Vegas, the first time I saw you lose in Philadelphia, Mississippi. I didn't say a word. I just shook my head and felt better believing you were worse off in your addiction than I was. Did you ever see me limping around the casino? Did you ever want to tell me to come home?

When the hollowness of winning and losing at Vassar for a decade got to be too much, and my body would not let me

213

push it hard or far enough, it fell in love with the attention of tired casino dealers who pitied, prodded, and resented.

Always in that order.

After I lost nearly all the money I had on blackjack tables, I usually sat in front of slot machines, looking over both shoulders at folk watching me pray to flirtatious contraptions programmed to pilfer. Slot machines made twinkly promises to me in the language of bonuses, big wins, jackpots, and hits. If they made good on their promises, I loved them. If they did not, I hated them.

I watched strangers frame crooked smiles when I won. I watched strangers frame crooked smiles when I lost. Like you, I did not know how to win. I'm not even sure I came to the casino to win. "You up or down?" was the extent of the conversation with folk I called "my casino friends." They didn't know my name. I didn't know theirs. They knew how I held my body when disgusted with what I'd made it do. I knew the same thing about them. "I'm here because I'm sad, lonely, and addicted to losing," is a sentence never shared between casino friends.

I kept coming back to the casino because I felt emptier and heavier when I lost than when I won. I couldn't win, because if I didn't have enough to begin with, I could never win enough to stop. And if I won, I came back to win more. And if I came back to win more, I would eventually lose. And after I eventually lost, I would remember the thrill of winning. No matter what, I would always come back with the stated intention of winning, and the unstated intention of harming myself. Still, in a place where there were no metal detectors, where liquor was free, where money was being taken in mass quantities, and most people were losing, I wondered why there wasn't more visible violence.

Flora Wadley never stepped foot in a casino before meeting me. She came to Vassar as an assistant professor four years after I started as an adjunct professor. Flora was brilliant and bold enough to still love *Moesha, The Parkers, Girlfriends,* Jane Austen, Zora Neale Hurston, and *Jem and the Holograms.* But she never wanted to be the black Hologram. She wanted to be Black Jem. Like me, she grew up with a young, single black mother. Like me, she loved school. Unlike me, she lost her mother at ten years old. One morning Flora went to elementary school in Hartford, Connecticut, forty miles from the casino. A little before noon, someone came to her class and told her that her mother had died. She spent the rest of her life knowing the people you valued most could never abandon you if you always prepared to be abandoned. Flora did not expect to win, but she worked every moment I knew her to make sure losing hurt as little as possible.

The first time Flora and I went to the casino, we didn't go to get away from work as much as to go somewhere shiny where we could hold hands. We'd put each other through hell and we were really trying to see if the relationship was something we should commit more time and energy to. We got a free hotel. We got free slot play. We didn't spend a dime of our own money. We went home happy.

But as we stressed about tenure, health, book deals, work, and family, lies between us came more frequently. We thought leaving Vassar was the only way to leave the lies. Instead, we moved onto campus in dorm apartments where we were expected to be available to kids who needed professorial support. Flora lived on one side of the dorm. I lived on the other. We didn't have to pay rent, bills, or for food. For the first time in our lives, all of our money earned was ours and we could pay off all of our student loans, all of our debts. We didn't imagine for a second that there would be a price to pay for going to sleep and waking up at work.

One day, on Flora's birthday, I decided to "really gamble." That meant I brought three hundred dollars to spend. Before long, that three hundred grew to six hundred. Then that six hundred gradually disappeared. Flora put that last seventy-five-dollar voucher in a machine and pressed three. She thought she was playing three dollars. The machine was a twenty-five-dollar machine and her seventy-five-dollar bet turned into a $6,700 win.

We thought we were rich.

Later that night, we won another four thousand and we left the casino up twelve thousand from when we came. I sent a large bit of my half to you and Grandmama. Flora used her half to pay down her credit card bill and student loans. I came back almost every weekend trying to win twelve thousand again. Once, I won fourteen thousand. Another time I won six thousand.

One Sunday I lost everything we came with. And I took out more money. And I lost that. Then we got a "free" hotel room so we could wait until midnight, when I could take out more money.

And I lost that.

I lost all of my savings and went home hateful of casinos and Flora for not making us leave. Whenever I thought about not going back, I let the casino lure my body back with free slot play or concert tickets or free rooms. Every time they offered me something, I went. And I lost. When I lost, I wanted to leave with something, so I used the "points" or comps I'd accumulated losing money to buy what amounted to free eight-thousand-dollar casino Pumas, free three-thousand-dollar casino dresses, free fourteen-hundred-dollar casino T-shirts, and free two-thousand-dollar seats to see Beyoncé, Kanye, Jigga, Sade, Prince, and Janelle Monáe.

I ate free casino veggie burgers, casino grilled cheeses, casino fries, casino onion rings, casino shakes when we arrived, and a nice dinner of free Mexican or Italian food later. After I lost all our money for the night, I ordered room service and ate free casino omelets and casino pancakes before watching Suze Orman until I fell asleep. This was the life I tried to drag Flora into every weekend after I lost all my savings. Flora mostly said no. Three times, she said yes. Whether I lost every dime I walked in with, or won more than I ever imagined, I always punished myself with casino food as ferociously as I'd punished myself with starving and exercising.

Once, when I was watching you spend your last dollar in a slot, I saw you reach in your purse, get your phone, and start texting. A minute later, I got this text from you:

I am so proud of you and your accomplishments. Some of those terrible people threw everything they could at you and never realized your fight has always been bigger than tenure. Forgive them, son. They know not what they do. It has never been our job to take out the trash. That kind of trash takes care of itself. The family is sorry you're alone up there. We thank you for your generosity and we wish you lots of love, joy, and health. God is good.

I read the text and realized there was nothing sadder than knowing we saw each other in a casino fourteen hundred miles from a home we shared, and neither of us had it in us to say hello, I miss you, stop, or let's go home.

Instead of leaving the casino, I sat next to a Korean American doctor who told me she lost her house, her cars, her children's tuition. She'd gone to Gamblers Anonymous twice, and tried dealing in the casino just to be around the gaming. She saved a lot of money, then lost it all again. I gave the woman the last hundred dollars in my pocket. She promised she was going home with it. I knew she was lying. After she left, a white man sat down at her machine and hit a jackpot. When he was waiting to be paid out, he said, "I wish they'd give Americans first dibs on these machines. The Asians are taking over the damn place. Seems like they win every other jackpot."

"Take over deez nuts," I told the white man, and walked my sad ass out of the casino.

The last time I saw you was the next-to-last time I was at the Connecticut casino with Flora Wadley. On the way home, Flora Wadley said the problem with our relationship was the casino.

I said the problem with us was us.

Flora said even if the problem was us, we could save our money if we stopped going to the casino and traveled somewhere fun every weekend.

I said we could enjoy traveling to those places more if we addressed what in us made us want to go to the casino in the first place. Flora said talking about trauma was traumatizing for her since her mother and grandmother died.

I said okay.

She said our choices have to be more than traumatizing each other at home or driving two hours to be traumatized and broke.

I said okay.

She suggested we go to counseling.

I said okay.

The one time we went to counseling, I didn't talk about the casino. I didn't talk about you. I didn't talk about my lies, my memory, my failed relationships, or my body. I talked about Flora. And Flora talked about Flora. And the counselor talked about Flora. And we got some homework to help us with our relationship to Flora's supposed deficiencies. And I threw that homework away the next day. And Flora threw that homework away a few days after that.

I got paid on the twenty-fifth of every month. I sent a fifth of my check to Grandmama and spent the rest of that check by the thirtieth at the casino. When my money was gone, I started getting payday loans. Flora had no idea what I was doing. I'd get a loan for thirteen hundred dollars on the fifteenth of every month. They'd take twenty-one hundred out of my account on payday. I sold my truck for sixteen thousand and gambled away every single dime of that money in one weekend. When I got paid, I rented cars and drove two and a half hours to give away my entire paycheck. A few months after gambling away my truck, I sold my leather living room set for two thousand dollars less than what we paid for it, and I gambled that five hundred dollars away in less than three minutes. I was a new kind of sick. I was an old kind of sick. I couldn't run but I could gamble.

And I could promise.

The Saturday after the cop told me he wanted me to take a polygraph test, I begged Flora to drive me to the casino. She made me promise that I wouldn't lose all of my money.

I promised.

We were there for half an hour before I lost my paycheck. Before driving home, we found a scratch-off in the back of her Kia worth five dollars. We took money from the scratch-off and went back to the casino. That five dollars turned into ten. Then a hundred. Then twelve hundred. Then thirty-six hundred. We went to bed in the casino that night happy that our persistence paid off, but we weren't happy enough to touch or leave.

I woke up that Sunday morning and kept gambling. Before I knew it, I had over ten thousand dollars. By this point, we both knew that there were no good gamblers. There were people who left when they were up and never came back, and there were people who did not. We decided that day to be people who left when we were up and never come back. With ten thousand dollars in my camouflage cargo shorts pocket, we got in Flora's Kia and headed home. A half mile from the casino, with thoughts of being stuck in a tiny apartment across the street from Vassar in our heads, I asked Flora if she thought I could hit again.

"I think you're hot," she said.

"You think I'm hot?"

"I think you're hot."

We turned around and went back to the casino. You were there. I should have asked you if you wanted to come home with us.

It took one hour to lose every cent of that ten thousand dollars.

I was not hot.

When we got home, I told Flora I was sorry for dragging her into my mess. She asked me to promise I'd never step one foot in that casino again.

I promised.

I apologized.

We hugged.

We cried.

We dried off each other's cheeks.

I walked into Flora's office, got ten dollars I'd seen hidden in between her books, and asked her if I could drive her Kia around Poughkeepsie just to clear my head. When she said yes, I got on the Taconic, merged onto Interstate 84, and headed back to the casino.

I texted you and asked if we could meet at the casino. I didn't tell you I needed help. I didn't tell you I was scared. I hadn't spent the night in the same bedroom with you in thirty years. I hadn't visited you in close to six years. I had no idea how much I weighed.

I walked into the casino with ten dollars in my pocket, wearing wrinkled camouflaged shorts, a thin 3X black hoodie, no socks, and black Adidas. I knew you'd hate my outfit. That's part of why I wore it every single day to teach the last four years.

I walked onto the casino floor intent on flipping my ten dollars into a few hundred before you got to the casino when I saw you sitting in front of your favorite game. You didn't know I was watching you. I walked upstairs to a free hotel room I was able to reserve because I was technically a "very important person" at the casino. I wondered how many "very important people" at the casino only had ten stolen dollars to their names.

When I got to the room, I stared at the space between the two queen beds, between the two small bottles of water, between the gigantic television and the massive window, between this huge man-made lake on the other side of the window and me.

You should have been up here thirty minutes ago, I told myself. My stomach hurt at the thought of having the first honest conversation of our lives. I walked out of the room and called to tell you not to come. Halfway down the hall, here you came wearing a thin yellow flowery scarf and toting a white plastic bag under your arm. "I brought you a hat," you said, and hugged my neck. You smelled like smoke, black soap, and thick hair grease. I asked if you were downstairs gambling before you came up. "You told me you liked the hat I got you for Christmas. Not trying to fight, Kie," you said, ignoring my question. "You stopped exercising completely, didn't you? Too much weight on an already heavy body is a recipe for disaster."

I ignored your statements about my body and asked what you would think if I moved back to Mississippi.

"Would you be moving back without a job?" you asked me. "Has Vassar asked you to leave? Why would you consider going backward after all you've been through in Mississippi? Promise me you won't do that. Can you tell me why you gained so much weight?"

I promised and ignored your question about my body. Without missing a beat, you continued, "Can I ask you a question?"

"You know you can ask me a question."

"Do you think I talk down to people? I'm asking because this woman at my new job said I make her and the other women in the office feel small. They're all liberal white women, and I just never thought that's what I have been doing."

I told you that I've been telling you that for years.

"I just didn't know that's how people saw me," you said. "That's a horrible way to interact with people. What do you want to say to me, Kie?"

"I guess I just want to know why."

"Why what?"

"Why?"

I sat on the foot of the bed. You sat at the desk. We looked at each other for minutes without saying a word. I knew you thought I was blaming you for something. I wasn't. To blame you, I'd have to admit to you how sad I was and how much I failed.

"This is not an excuse," you said before standing up and grabbing my hand. "When I was your age, you were fifteen years old. Can you imagine going through whatever you're going through with a fifteen-year-old black child in Jackson, Mississippi?"

"No," I said. "I can't."

"You were a hardheaded child running toward an early death, or prison. I still worry that you're running toward an early death or prison. I think that's part of why you've gotten so heavy again. The truth is I just didn't know how to protect you."

"But why?"

"Why what?"

"Just why?" I asked you.

"We never told the truth, Kie," you said. "No one in our family has ever told the truth."

"I told you the truth."

"Until you started resenting me for what happened with Malachi?"

"That's not what happened."

223

"That is what happened," you said. "You did not tell me the truth, Kie. Say it."

"The truth about what?"

"The truth about anything. You haven't told me the truth about why you gained all your weight back. You haven't told me the truth about your romantic relationships. You haven't told me the truth about your job. I think you've done that as a way of punishing me. When we do talk on the phone, you raise your voice. You won't get a grip. Honestly, I think that's abusive."

I looked at you and waited for more words to come out of your mouth. When nothing else came out, I told you that I was sorry for lying to you. I lied to you, sometimes because I did not know how to tell you the truth, sometimes because I did not understand the truth, other times because I did not think you could hold the truth. Every time I lied, I wanted to control you, control your memory of us, control your vision of me. I was afraid to talk about being emotionally abusive, about gorging, about starving, about gambling all my money away, about wanting to disappear. I didn't talk with you about those days at Beulah Beauford's house, about what my body felt in the bedrooms of our house in Jackson. I didn't think there was any way you could love me if I really showed you more of who, and what, and where I'd been.

So I did what we do.

I told you the truth about white folks' treatment of me without being honest about how I treated myself and others close to me while surviving that treatment.

After you hugged my neck, said you were so sorry, and asked questions about what the officers did to me in the interrogation room, I said, "Wait. So I abused you?" just loud enough for the people in the room next door to hear.

"I think so."

"I abused you by lying to you? Did you abuse me?"

You stood up and walked toward the door. "Do you ever just feel lonely? I feel like I walk around this world raw, Kie. It's hard to open up when you're already open, and people just never get tired of sticking their nasty hands into that raw."

"I hear you," I said, "but I'm asking if you abused me. How did I stick my hands into your raw? How did I abuse you?"

"You come from that raw, Kie. I think you're raw, too. I know you love me. I just think you share too much with people who don't love either of us. You let too many hands into that raw. There are things I want to say to you that white folk do not deserve to hear. I have a heart, Kie. I have a heart and a job. And even though you don't act like it, you do, too. You've got to be much more careful. White folk do not deserve to stick their nasty hands into our raw. Hiding from them and being excellent are actually the only ways for us to survive here."

I told you that running and hiding from folk who can't see themselves has fatal consequences. You told me that unnecessarily opening yourself up for folk who can't see themselves has even more fatal consequences. I asked you why we're still talking about people not in this room.

"Because they're listening, Kie," you said. "They read everything you write. They see how you dress. They are watching. You make it easy for white folk to discredit you. You really think you're free. It's one of the most endearing things about you. But every single time they remind you what you really are, you crumble and lie about that crumbling. I just want you to protect yourself."

"Protect myself from who?"

"You mean 'from whom.' I'm still trying to protect you from them, from the world. I failed at that."

I told you that I never crumbled, and asked if I should have done anything to protect myself from you.

"You did protect yourself from me," you said, and looked toward the door for the second time in the conversation. "You know what it feels like to have people ask me why my only son never visits me, doesn't pick up the phone when I call, doesn't respond to e-mails?"

"No," I said. "That's not what I know."

"Kie," you finally said. "I'm just asking you to forgive me for whatever I've done to make you this resentful."

Now I'm hunting for the other side of that door. A casino is no place to ask a parent or child drowning in shame why they were abusive. "Can we just not lie?" I asked. "I'm really asking. Can we start there? Can we just promise each other we won't lie?"

You buried your head in your chest. You picked up your bag and walked toward the door. You turned around, walked back to me. You stood over me while I sat on the edge of the bed. I looked up at your face. My body remembered, but my body did not flinch. My body did not shudder. My body did not brace. I wanted you to kneel down and hold my face in your hands. I wanted you to say let's please be honest about where we've been. I wanted you to be gentle. I wanted to remember being your child.

"Can we just not lie?"

"Yes, we can," you said. "I promise we can. Just know that I did the best I could, Kie. That's all I'm trying to say. I didn't know how to do any better. I did the best I could."

"But why do you need me to know that? What if you didn't do the best you could? What if you could have actually done better?"

"What do you mean?"

"I just think sometimes we don't do the best we could have done, and it's impossible to know that if we're scared to remember where we've been, and what we actually did. I don't think either of us did our best. I know I didn't. Do you really believe you did?"

You ignored my question and asked me why I write instead of paint or sing or dance or cook or sculpt. I told you that I write because you made me, and I write what I write because I am afraid of becoming you or my father. I told you that it took me ten years of teaching to understand that my students loved me, valued our time, but they did not want to become me. I told you that you cared so much for black folk, but couldn't believe there were some folk in this nation who could love you in the worst minutes of the worst hours of the worst days of your life. I told you that I was one of those folk. And Grandmama was, too.

I told you I imagine you at eleven years old, climbing Grandmama's pecan tree with *A Tale of Two Cities* in your hands. I see you reading, but I also see you looking down at Grandmama's pink shotgun house, watching your brother throw pecans at your two sisters. I see you watching Grandmama rock back and forth alone on that porch. Your eyes meet her eyes and Grandmama tells you to come on down from that tree before you fall and break your arm. You smile

227

because you know Grandmama just wants you and the rest of her children to be careful. You are curious. You are weird. You are loved. You are audacious. You are as safe as you'll ever be. Tomorrow, you and Grandmama know that you will all be less safe. Today, though, twenty minutes from Sunday school, tucked securely in a pecan tree with a book in your hand, you are free.

"I be seeing you," I told you, "especially when you think you be doing a great job of hiding. Maybe you be seeing me too."

You did not correct my English because it could not be corrected. You held my hand and we hugged for longer than we'd hugged in over thirty years. I was a grown man, but I was your child, and I fell in love again that day.

Hand in hand, we walked out of the hotel room. We stepped into an elevator. We walked across the casino lobby and made it outside the casino. You hugged my neck and told me you did not want to let go. I felt so free, so fantastic, so delivered.

"I want you to feel like I'm always home," you said. "Could you please get control of your weight? Will you go on a diet?"

"I will," I said.

"You promise?"

"I promise."

"I'm sorry for hurting you, Kie. Do you want to say anything else?"

"We all broken," I said. "Some broken folk do whatever they can not to break other folk. If we're gone be broken, I wonder if we can be those kind of broken folk from now on. I think it's possible to be broken and ask for help without breaking other people."

"I'm sorry for breaking you," you said.

"You didn't break me," I told you. "You helped make me. I helped make you. We can talk more honestly about that making. That's really all I'm saying. That's what people can do."

"I think we turned a page in our relationship today, Kie."

"You think so?" I asked you.

"I know we did," you said. "Please come visit me. Please stop eating so much sugar and so many carbs. You have one body. Please value it."

I watched you get in the taxi. The taxi door closed. You slowly disappeared on the other side of a winding curve. I'd parked Flora's Kia on the other side of the building, so I had to walk through the casino to get to the car. I did not make eye contact with the blackjack dealers. I did not say fuck you to the twinkling slot machines. I did not suck my teeth at the Johnny Rockets, Ben and Jerry's, and Krispy Kreme. I simply said bye to them and made it to Flora's Kia.

I knew this would be my last time in a casino.

Thank you for not giving up on me, you texted four minutes later.

Do not put any of your hard-earned money into those machines. Be better than me. I am going to get help. Please stop and smell the roses. Promise me you will lose weight.

I promise, I texted.

Consider getting married and having kids. You would be a great father. Your children would be so lucky. You are better than your parents' failures. Promise me you will consider getting married and having children this year.

I wanted to tell you that if I ever have a child, I want to raise that child in the Deep South. I want free land to wrap around that child's feet. I want that child to know that you do not need to be magical, or mythologize the so-called struggle. I am not at all sure what the child will need, but I want them to figure out the kind of lover of black children they want to be. And I want them to accept that we are all black children. I want them to articulate whether they are capable of being that kind of lover, and I want them to never wall themselves up from the world when they fail at loving themselves or our people.

I know that's a lot.

I wanted to tell you that I am afraid to bring a child into the world because I do not know how to protect my child from life, from you, from our nation, and from me. I worry about the possibility of our black child feeling my touch was violation. I wondered what our child would see when I was scared. I wondered what they'd hear when I was angry. I learned indirectly from you that we cannot responsibly love anyone, and especially not black children in America, if we insist on making a practice of hiding and running from ourselves. I wonder if a part of me wants to hold on to the possibility of hiding, running, and harming myself. I cannot do that if I have a child.

I did not have the courage to text you any of that. So instead I wrote, I promise. We've come too far to turn back.

We really have, you texted back. Promise me you will do what I asked. Promise me you will leave the past where it is and go forward with no regrets. Promise me you will not look back.

I promise, I texted. You are right. Tomorrow is the first day of the rest of our lives. I will try to bring a child into this world. I will teach that child to never look back. We cannot live healthy lives in the present if we drown ourselves in the past.

Promise me you mean everything you're saying, Kie.

I can't promise that.

Please promise, Kiese. Please.

For a few seconds, I remembered that the most abusive parts of our nation obsessively neglect yesterday while peddling in possibility. I remembered that we got here by refusing to honestly remember together. I remembered that it was easier to promise than it was to reckon or change. But I wanted to continue feeling delivered. I wanted to continue feeling fantastic. I wanted to continue feeling free. And I wanted to feel loved by both of us again.

I promise, I slowly texted. We have come too far to turn back. I promise. We have come way too far to turn back.

BEND

Two miles from all those promises and three minutes from our last cliché, I will understand that no meaningful promises are made or kept in casinos. I will head back to the casino and spend the last ten dollars I stole from Flora's apartment. I will stop at Vassar College when I leave the casino. I will not know where home is. I will not smell the roses. I will not leave the past in the past. I will teach my students. I will write and revise. I will become a tired teacher and a terrified black writer.

I will take a train to Washington, DC, to talk to the architects of Barack Obama's "My Brother's Keeper" initiative. I will argue, with a group of committed intersectional feminists, that we need effective structural remedies to structural impediments for black children in this country. We will argue that black girls and black women, like black men and boys, cannot wait. I will take the train back to Poughkeepsie with Flora feeling good about fighting for black girls and black women. On the way home, I will lie to Flora, a black woman, who lost her mother when she was a black girl. Flora will not forgive me.

I will continue to hide behind podiums, lecterns, huge camouflage shorts, and black sweatshirts. I will listen to you talk about addiction. I will say no when you ask me to wire you four thousand dollars tomorrow. I will punish myself for saying no by going to a casino and blowing my last four thousand dollars the day after tomorrow.

I will not know where home is.

I will hate going to sleep. I will hate waking up. I will not buy a gun because I know I will use it. I will watch them murder Tamir Rice's body for using his imagination outside. I will watch them call Toya Graham, a black mother who beat her son upside the head during the Baltimore rebellion, "Mom of the Year." I will watch them murder Korryn Gaines's body for using her voice and a gun to defend her five-year-old black child from America. I will watch them murder Philando Castile in front of his partner, Diamond Reynolds, and her child. I will watch, and hear, that black child tell her mother, another black child, "I don't want you to get shooted. I can keep you safe."

I can keep you safe.

I will watch them ridicule us and exonerate themselves for terrorizing the bodies of black children they have yet to shoot. I will hear them call themselves innocent, American, and Christian as they call us ungrateful, irresponsible, reckless, thuggish.

I will not buy a gun because I know I will use it.

I will watch Dougie, LaThon, Donnie Gee, Abby, Nzola, Ray Gunn, and scores of my students raise their children. I will avoid them all because I am ashamed of how heavy I've become and how childless I am. I will live and sleep alone, just like you. I will want to lie every day of my life, just like you. I will want to starve. I will want to gorge. I will want to punish my black body because fetishizing and punishing black bodies are what we are trained to do well in America.

I will write. I will revise.

When I finally decide to leave Vassar College, I will remember meeting *The College Dropout*; *A Mercy*; *K.R.I.T. Wuz Here*; *The Electric Lady*; *Prophets of the Hood*; *good kid, m.A.A.d city*; and *Salvage the Bones*. I will remember teaching and learning from the weirdest, most avidly curious students I'd ever imagined. I will apologize for failing them. I will understand that every single one of my colleagues at Vassar College tried to love, serve, and teach the students in front of them. And just like me, they often failed at loving, serving, and teaching the students in front of them.

I will find my way back to Mississippi to finish revising a book I started thirty years ago on Grandmama's porch. I will drive by Beulah Beauford's house, Millsaps College, St. Richard, St. Joe, LaThon's house, Jabari's house, Ray Gunn's apartment, Jackson State, Donnie Gee's house, familiar parking lots, grocery stores, interstates, basketball courts. I will walk slowly through rooms, scenes, smells, and sounds I made myself forget. While sitting on a porch in Oxford, Mississippi, I will hear Grandmama's voice tell me "Ain't nothing for you up in there" when I want to give my blessings away.

I will fall to my knees that day and laugh and I will laugh and I will laugh until I cry. I will drive to Forest and read a draft of this book to Grandmama from beginning to end on her porch. She will say, "I think it's real good, Kie" even though she will periodically fall asleep while I'm reading. "Thank you for all them words," she will say every time she wakes up. "And thank you for all y'all do for me."

Grandmama will ask me to wheel her back into the house after I finish reading and find that thirty-year-old raggedy gold and silver contraption she calls her phone book. "Gimme

your number again, Jimmy Earl," Grandmama will say, looking right in my face. "I tried to call you last night but I don't
believe I got the right number in here."

I will look in the phone book and show Grandmama my
number under *K*, not *J*.

"Oh, okay," she will say. "I already got the number, Kie?"
She will pick up the phone and start dialing the number she
had for Uncle Jimmy. "Jimmy Earl not answering," she will
say. "I reckon I'll call back in a little while."

I will not remind Grandmama how she found the body of
her first child, Jimmy Earl Alexander, dead on the floor of his
kitchen from an overdose a few years earlier. "Me and Jimmy
Earl," she will say, "we love talking to each other on that tele-
phone."

I will wonder about the memories Grandmama misplaced, forgot, or maybe just lost from the time I started
this book until I finished. I will wonder if the memories that
remain with age are heavier than the ones we forget because
they mean more to us, or if our bodies, like our nation, eventually purge memories we never wanted to be true. I will
wonder if at ninety years old, after remembering and carrying so much, Grandmama has any room left in her body for
new memories.

Though Grandmama confused me with Uncle Jimmy
during our conversation, she will remember that I am forty-
three years old, heavy, and childless. "It's still time for you to
be somebody's daddy and somebody's husband, Kie," she will
say. "What is it you scared of?"

I will smile and say I do not want to hurt anybody.

Grandmama will say she believes me even when she knows
I am lying. I will kneel down, hug her neck, and thank her for

responsibly loving all of her children, and never, ever harming me.

"I was just trying to put y'all where I been," she will say.

"I am just trying to put y'all where I bend," I will hear.

I will show Grandmama my first stretch mark and talk to her about how it's changed in thirty years. I will show her these six scratches on my right wrist from years of trying to dunk. I will show her a blotched scar underneath my right eye. I pull my bottom lip down and show her scar tissue from a fall. I will show her these three eyelashes on my left eye that curl downward instead of up. I will show her how my right big toe is so much more callused than my left one since I lost mobility in my left hip. I will show her the holes in my mouth where teeth would be if I thought my health was worth taking care of. I will show her how much softer my thighs have gotten over the years since I stopped trying to disappear. I will show her my wide palms and short fingers. I will show her my navel and the two new stretch marks framing it.

Grandmama will ask me if I am okay. "No," I will tell her. "I'm not sure any of us are okay."

Grandmama will hold me longer than she has ever held me and she will wail. She will tell me she hasn't really looked in the mirror in years because the black body she sees ain't the black body she remembers.

"It's your black body, though," I will tell her. "And you can remember your black body and all it's been through a whole lot of different ways."

"I don't know how to remember but one way," Grandmama will tell me.

"Now you lying, Grandmama," I will tell her. "You know you lying, too. You don't make it this far only knowing how to remember one way. You know I love you, but you lying right now."

Grandmama will laugh and laugh and laugh until she tells me she is sorry. I will not have the courage to ask her what she is apologizing for.

But I will know.

I will remember that I am your child. And, really, you are mine. And we are Grandmama's. And Grandmama is ours. You will tell me that you regret ever beating, manipulating, or demeaning me. You will tell me that you regret punishing yourself when you were lonely, shameful, and afraid.

I will remind you that I did not write this book to you simply because you are a black woman, or deeply southern, or because you taught me how to read and write. I wrote this book to you because, even though we harmed each other as American parents and children tend to do, you did everything you could to make sure the nation and our state did not harm their most vulnerable children. I will tell you that white folk and white power often helped make me feel gross, criminal, angry, and scared as a child, but they could never make me feel intellectually incapable because I was your child.

You gave your students and me more than the gifts of writing, revision, reading, and rereading. That's what I want you to know as you close this book. You modeled a rugged love of Mississippi. You insisted our liberation has its bedrock in compassion, organization, imagination, and direct action. You proselytized home training. You demanded that we develop a radical moral imagination. I finally understand revision, rereading, compassion, home training, imagination, and a love of black children are the greatest gifts any American can share with any child in this nation. You taught us to give our lives and work to the liberation of black children in this country. I am working on that, and I finally understand there can be no liberation when our most intimate relationships are built on—and really inflected by—deception, abuse, misdirection, antiblackness, patriarchy, and bald-faced lies. Not teaching me this would have been the gravest kind of abuse.

I will offer you my heart. I will offer you my head. I will offer you my body, my imagination, and my memory. I will ask you to give us a chance at a more meaningful process of healing. If we fall, give us a chance to fall honestly, compassionately together. The nation as it is currently constituted has never dealt with a yesterday or tomorrow where we were radically honest, generous, and tender with each other.

It will, though. It will not be reformed. It will be bent, broken, undone, and rebuilt. The work of bending, breaking, and building the nation we deserve will not start or end with you or me; but that work will necessitate loving black family, however oddly shaped, however many queer, trans, cis, and gender-nonconforming mamas, daddies, aunties, comrades, nieces, nephews, granddaddies, and grandmamas—learning how to talk, listen, organize, imagine, strategize, and fight fight fight for and with black children.

There will always be scars on, and in, my body from where you harmed me. You will always have scars on, and in, your body from where we harmed you. You and I have nothing and everything to be ashamed of, but I am no longer ashamed of this heavy black body you helped create. I know that our beautiful bruised black bodies are where we bend.

I will send a draft of the book to you when I think it's done. I will take out some of what you say needs to be taken out. I will not ignore your questions about my weight. I will not punish myself. I will not misdirect or manipulate human beings, regardless of their age, especially those human beings who love me enough to risk being misdirected or manipulated. I will not misdirect or manipulate myself. I will not say I am naked when I am fully clothed. I will not say I am sorry when I am resentful. I will not give my blessings away. I will love myself enough to be honest when I fail at loving. I will accept that black children will not recover from economic inequality, housing discrimination, sexual violence, heteropatriarchy, mass incarceration, mass evictions, and parental abuse. I will accept that black children are all worthy of the most abundant, patient, responsible kind of love and liberation this world has ever created. And we are worthy of sharing the most abundant, patient, responsible kind of love and liberation with every vulnerable child on this planet.

We will find churches, synagogues, mosques, and porches committed to the love, liberation, memories, and imagination of black children. We will share. We will find psychologists committed to the love, liberation, memories, and imagination of black children. We will share. We will find teachers committed to the love, liberation, memories, and imagination of black children. We will share. We will find healers committed to the love, liberation, memories, and imagination of black children. We will share. We will find art communities, co-operatives, curriculums, justice and labor organizations committed to the love, memories, and imagination of black children. We will share. We will remember, imagine, and help create what we cannot find.

Or, it is possible we will not remember.

We will not imagine.

We will not share.

We will not swing back.
We will not organize.
We will not be honest.
We will not be tender.
We will not be generous.
We will do what Americans do.
We will abuse like Americans abuse.
We will forget like Americans forget.
We will hunt like Americans hunt.
We will hide like Americans hide.
We will love like Americans love.
We will lie like Americans lie.
We will die like Americans die.
We did not ever have to be this way.
We will not ever have to be this way.

I wanted to write a lie. You wanted to read a lie. I wrote this to you instead because I am your child, and you are mine. You are also my mother and I am your son. Please do not be mad at me, Mama. I am just trying to put you where I bend. I am just trying to put us where we bend.